W9-AZF-018

TIME FOR KIDS

Start Exploring
Nonfiction Reading in Mathematics

SHELL EDUCATION

Credits

Editors
Christina Hill, M.A.
Conni Medina

Assistant Editor
Leslie Huber, M.A.

Senior Editor
Lori Kamola, M.A.Ed.

Editor-in-Chief
Sharon Coan, M.S.Ed.

Editorial Manager
Gisela Lee, M.A.

Creative Director
Lee Aucoin

Cover Design
Robin Erickson

Illustration Manager/Designer
Timothy J. Bradley

Interior Layout Design
Robin Erickson

Print Production
Phil Garcia

Publisher
Corinne Burton, M.A.Ed.

Shell Education
5301 Oceanus Drive
Huntington Beach, California 92649
1-877-777-3450
http://www.shelleducation.com

ISBN 978-1-4258-0453-4

© 2008 Shell Education

Learning Standards: Copyright 2004 McREL. www.mcrel.org/standards-benchmarks.

The classroom teacher may reproduce copies of materials in this book for classroom use only. The reproduction of any part for an entire school or school system is strictly prohibited. No part of this publication may be transmitted, stored, or recorded in any form without written permission from the publisher.

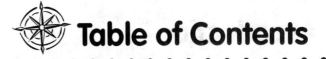

Table of Contents

Introduction

How to Use This Product

Start Exploring Nonfiction Reading in Mathematics has been designed to enhance your reading program. The activities will motivate students to want to read with **high-interest**, **nonfiction content** and **engaging photographs**. Moreover, the authentic nonfiction reading experiences these activities provide can help students develop **vocabulary**, **comprehension**, and **fluency** skills in accordance with Reading First legislation. Within each unit of study, you will find easy-to-follow lesson plans and reading comprehension strategies ideal for your Pre-K, kindergarten, and first grade students. Each lesson is correlated to both Pre-K and K–2 standards. For more information, see Correlation to Standards (pages 19–21).

Each unit includes a set of activity cards based on a theme. The four themes in this book are **Numbers**, **Operations**, **Sort and Clasify**, and **Time and Money**. Each card includes activities for **activating prior knowledge**, **skills for language development**, and new ideas for **building knowledge and comprehension**. These activities are especially important for ELL and below-level students. The activity cards can be taught separately or in conjunction with the lessons. The lessons provide ideas for teaching the cards in a variety of ways, including whole-class lessons and small-group centers.

Each unit contains **two introductory lessons** that teach specific reading comprehension skills, followed by **focus lessons** and **centers** to **reinforce students' comprehension**. The **wrap-up lesson** found at the end of each unit combines and reinforces the skills taught throughout the unit. The **student reproducible pages** (found at the end of each unit) are used for practice and comprehension. These pages are usually distributed during one of the center activities. Also, consider using the activity sheets as assessments for reading comprehension.

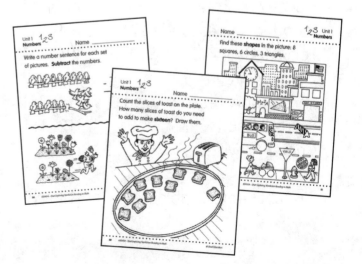

Research

Academic Readiness

The current thrust of education spending in the No Child Left Behind Act is academic readiness. This sweeping legislation places greater emphasis on language acquisition and early reading development in preschool and the primary grades. Research supports the belief that reading success by third grade leads to later academic success (U.S. Department of Education 2000).

Young children's early reading and writing proficiency is, therefore, an area of great interest both to policy makers and early-childhood professionals. The Early Reading First guidelines (U.S. Department of Education 2001) in No Child Left Behind include a program goal emphasizing the following:

- Oral language
- Phonological awareness
- Print awareness
- Alphabetic knowledge

A report from the National Institute of Child Health and Human Development, widely known as the Report of the National Reading Panel (2000), has generated new research in early reading. Despite the reading research base drawn on by the National Reading Panel, questions about young children's literacy development persist. How do children first begin to use written language? What can classroom teachers do to help all children be successful in unlocking the alphabetic principle and the code system of written language?

Early reading is an interwoven web of experiences, one part of which is children's early exposure to print in their world. Supplementing and enriching the curriculum with activities using familiar print provides an "auditory and visual anchor to remember letter symbol and sound" (Christie et al. 2002). By including activities with environmental print (the print found in a child's natural environment), teachers can provide opportunities for children to connect their prior knowledge to literacy experiences in school. Such experiences with familiar print assist children with word recognition and provide them with a sense of ownership when they recognize product logos and product labels that they see in their communities every day.

This book will guide the early childhood educator with a variety of ideas for enriching an existing comprehensive integrated curriculum for young children with environmental-print connections. You will find that encounters with environmental-print activities assist children in making connections between literacy experiences they encounter in their personal lives and those they learn at school.

Learning to Read

Early childhood educators have much to consider as they negotiate instructional strategies in their own classroom settings. Decades of research suggest that children start developing early literacy skills through their day-to-day experiences in a print-rich literate society (Berry 2001; Christie, Enz, and Vukelich 2002; Ferreiro and Teberosky 1982; Goodman 1986; Harste, Burke, and Woodward 1982). Children's prior knowledge of print in the environment—signs, billboards, logos, and functional print that saturate their world—can be used by teachers to make a meaningful bridge between what children already know and what they encounter in the school curriculum (Christie et al. 2002;

Introduction

Research *(cont.)*

Duke and Purcell-Gates 2003; Orellana and Hernandez 2003; Xu and Rutledge 2003). Purposeful planned encounters with environmental print can assist children in making connections between print in the home, print in the community, and school literacy experiences. Teachers can assist young children to become proficient readers and writers in many ways. The National Association for the Education of Young Children (2001) suggests the integrated use of speaking, listening, reading, and writing in the following ways:

- Provide social experiences for using language purposefully.
- Use reading and speaking to support oral language and vocabulary development.
- Use the home language and culture to introduce new words and concepts.
- Build on children's experiences.
- Provide opportunities to write.
- Play with language to develop phonemic awareness.
- Build knowledge of letters, sounds, and words.

This book provides opportunities for students to participate in all of these activities.

Simmons, Gunn, Smith, and Kame'enui (1994) stress the importance of teaching letters and sounds for reading success. They suggest the teaching of phonemic awareness through segmenting and blending sounds. While the awareness of sound units in phonemes, syllables, and words is a strong indicator of later reading success, keep in mind that, above all, reading is a meaning-making process. Letter and sound correspondences are beginning components of learning to read, but the comprehension of text is why children learn to read. The preteaching activities provided for each card provide opportunities for students to work on phonemic awareness skills.

Satisfaction and enjoyment, the power of human interaction, the communication of important messages, pleasure and delight in the words themselves, along with the ability to match letters to sounds, overlay the skills of decoding. Phonemic awareness, the knowledge of rhyming, blending, and segmenting of letter sounds, serves as knowledge only if embedded in meaningful experiences. It is the responsibility of educators to provide meaningful experiences for students. As you complete the activities in this book with your students, you will be providing students with these meaningful experiences.

Refer to the References Cited (page 170) for a complete list of the sources used to create this book.

Best Practices: Learning to Read

Reading Readiness

All students need a good foundation in basic developmental areas such as language, cognition, motor development, social and emotional development, and self-help. Many early childhood classrooms include students with chronological ages from four to six years old. Developmentally, this could mean huge differences in readiness skills and abilities within one classroom. To help prepare all students for emergent reading and writing curriculums, certain objectives need to be taught when students first begin school.

Twelve of the reading-readiness objectives include the following:

1. Students recite their own name.

2. Students recognize their own names in writing.

3. Students demonstrate an understanding of left-to-right progression (moving hand and eyes across a page left to right).

4. Students understand the concepts of *same* and *different*.

5. Students match, sort, and classify objects, pictures, and shapes that have common properties.

6. Students understand rhyming words.

7. Students understand the concept of *opposite*.

8. Students understand the concept of *sequencing*.

9. Students can express themselves in complete sentences.

10. Students demonstrate phonemic awareness (understanding that sounds are the building blocks for our language).

11. Students can identify alphabet letters.

12. Students demonstrate phonics awareness (understanding that language sounds have written symbols).

The twelve objectives listed above are just some of the reading-readiness skills recommended as a foundation for an emergent, lifelong reader. Other factors that are as important include attention span, emotional maturity, and language experiences.

A well-balanced early childhood program includes many of these objectives and supports a learning environment enriched with literacy activities. *Start Exploring Nonfiction Reading in Mathematics* can assist teachers in providing this type of environment. Nonfiction text that stimulates language development and student participation can help children at all levels become beginning readers and writers. Since the lessons have already been prepared and organized, hours of teacher and parent preparation time can be used instead for important student guidance and teaching time.

Introduction

Best Practices:
Learning to Read (cont.)

Interactive Reading Steps

The following steps provide effective reading strategies to help students improve their reading skills.

Modeled Reading

When a teacher reads out loud with enthusiasm and fluency, this provides students with a modeled reading lesson. Students make predictions about the story being read, discuss together facts about the main characters and events, and share their own subject-related experiences. The purpose of this type of reading is to foster a desire to read. It also helps enrich students' vocabulary and enhances their knowledge of the world around them. It is recommended that both fiction and nonfiction be read aloud to students on a daily basis.

Shared Reading

During shared reading times, the teacher and students read together from the same book, song, or poem. Shared reading often involves repetition and helps students connect to stories in a nonthreatening atmosphere. Students increase their vocabulary and learn to problem-solve and predict in a group setting. Shared reading helps promote independent reading. Small mini-books that students create are also great tools to use for shared reading. All the books have the same words and are often related to the thematic unit being studied.

Guided Reading

During guided reading, the teacher works with students who are grouped by ability levels. The students read the same simple story and feel successful because the reading material has been chosen to meet their needs and abilities. In such groups, students build self-confidence by sharing information they read about and by successfully understanding the material they are reading. They answer problem-solving questions about the material and are given several opportunities to respond. Overall, these types of groups strengthen the students' thinking skills.

Independent Reading

During independent reading, students read materials for practice and enjoyment. They choose high-interest books that help promote fluency and responsibility for their own learning. In the beginning, these materials often contain simple text and repetitive language. Most of the books, poems, and charts for independent reading are texts the students have already been exposed to several times during the modeled-, shared-, and guided-reading sessions.

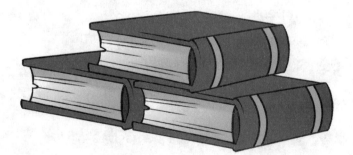

Best Practices:
Learning to Read *(cont.)*

Language Development

Long before students are introduced to written words, reading skills are being developed. Practicing oral language is a vital reading-readiness skill. There are several ways to bring excellent language development activities into a classroom environment. Here are some suggestions that could be used to enhance student vocabulary, self-esteem, and language acquisition:

- reading out loud to the students (nonfiction and fiction material)
- repetitive language in big books with student participation
- specific sharing times for students
- reciting poetry and singing thematic songs
- puppetry
- books with tapes at listening centers
- partner visiting times
- whole-class brainstorming sessions and discussions
- journal dictations
- "big buddy" activities (cross-age tutors)
- book sharing with "adopted grandparents"
- dramatization of short plays, poems, and stories
- monthly videotaping sessions
- dress-up area in the classroom
- student/teacher conversations
- storytelling
- class "visiting times" during centers or free play
- educational videos
- "Star (or Person) of the Week" sharing
- flag salute (explanation of words)

Introduction

Best Practices: The Five Components of Reading

The Report of the National Reading Panel marked a qualitative shift in beginning reading and writing instruction across the United States (National Institute of Child Health and Human Development 2000). It has generated new early reading standards, curriculum approaches, and classroom practices. The No Child Left Behind legislation has taken the outcomes of the National Reading Panel (NRP) report and translated these into very specific Reading First guidelines. These guidelines specify that instructional programs be based on valid scientific research and address the learning needs of all students, including high and low achievers, English language learners, and special education students. The guidelines further specify the five essential components in high-quality reading instruction that emerged from the Report of the National Reading Panel: 1. Phonemic Awareness, 2. Phonics, 3. Fluency, 4. Comprehension, 5. Vocabulary.

Phonemic awareness instruction should provide explicit instruction that focuses on letter-sound relationships, segmenting, and blending. The Reading First guidelines look for early linkage between sounds and letter symbols, even before letter names are learned, as well as ongoing assessment of phonemic awareness skills to inform instruction.

Phonics and word study instruction, according to the National Reading Panel, should also be explicit and systematic and teach letter-sound connections and blending skills to read whole words. These same skills must be applied to learning to spell. Reading text demands that students immediately apply their phonics knowledge to decode and comprehend what is being read. And, as with phonemic awareness instruction, phonics and word study skills must be systematically assessed to inform continued instruction.

Fluency instruction appears in the NRP report as an essential component of reading. The Reading First guidelines call for opportunities for oral repeated reading that is supported by the teacher, by peers, and at home by family members. The text that students read and reread should be well matched to their reading skills and should build rate and accuracy of oral reading.

Comprehension instruction, not surprisingly, appears in the NRP report as an essential component of reading instruction. This must include teaching before, during, and after reading both narrative and informational text. Teachers must explicitly explain and model strategies that aid comprehension. Discussion techniques and questioning strategies must also be directly explained and modeled by the teacher. Extended opportunities must be provided to struggling readers—low readers, English language learners, and special-needs students—to participate in successful reading experiences.

Vocabulary instruction is the fifth component of the NRP report. Vocabulary instruction, according to Reading First guidelines, must also be direct, systematic, and explicit. The meanings of words and word-learning strategies must be taught by the teacher. Structural analysis of words and the etymology of words must be taught as well.

Best Practices: The Five Components of Reading *(cont.)*

Phonemic Awareness

Phonemic awareness refers to a person's ability to attend to and manipulate the sounds of spoken words. In order to begin reading, a child needs to understand that words are made up of individual sounds. As described in the Report of the National Reading Panel, there are several elements involved in phonemic awareness instruction. These include phoneme isolation, phoneme identification, phoneme categorization, phoneme blending, phoneme segmentation, phoneme deletion, phoneme addition, and phoneme substitution. This book provides lessons and activities to draw attention to the sounds that make up words. Students need to have a strong understanding of the spoken language before they can understand the written language. Sounds are the building blocks of language. Students must first have phonemic awareness before phonics can make sense to them. There is first an awareness of spoken words, then syllables, onsets, and rimes. The definitions below are important for any teacher or parent to understand when working with students at the early childhood level.

- *Phonemic awareness* is being able to hear the sounds that make up words, see relationships between these sounds, and create or rearrange sounds to create new words.
- *Phoneme* is an individual sound; for example, "t" is a phoneme and so is "ow."
- *Onset* is the beginning sound or sounds before the first vowel. In *cat* "c" is the onset. In *stop* "st" is the onset.
- *Rime* is the first vowel and the rest of the word. The rime in *man* is "an." The rime in *stand* is "and."

- *Phonics* is the process of associating sounds with written symbols. Phonics gives students word attack skills for sounding out and blending letter sounds in written words.

Note: Both phonemic awareness and phonics are needed to help students develop word recognition skills.

A balanced literacy approach combines phonemic awareness, phonics, sight words, vocabulary development, comprehension, and fluency into an enriched learning environment for emergent readers and authors. Students themselves help to create such an environment by using natural and functional written language. For example, students may help dictate "Rules for Taking Care of Our Pet Fish." There might also be a post office in the classroom where students can draw pictures and write letters to each other. A content rich environment integrates science, social studies, math, and the arts to make learning more meaningful for students.

Phonemic Awareness Activities

Thumbs Up, Thumbs Down (Identifying Identical and Differing Phoneme Structures)

Tell students you are going to say two words. If the two are the same word, students should show thumbs up. If the two are not the same word, students should show thumbs down. Demonstrate several words for the students until they understand the task. For example, if you said the words *cap – cap*, students should indicate they are the same word by showing thumbs up. If you said the words *cap – tap*, students should indicate they are not the same word by showing thumbs down.

Introduction

Best Practices: The Five Components of Reading *(cont.)*

Phoneme Count (Counting Phonemes)

Students are to determine how many sounds they hear in a word and then clap one time for each sound. For example, if you say the word *sun*, students should determine there are three sounds and clap three times.

If students have difficulty determining the number of sounds, help them analyze the word by segmenting it. For example, after saying the word *sun*, segment the word by saying /s/ pause /u/ pause /n/. In this way, students will have an easier time determining the different sounds.

Mystery Word (Phoneme Blending)

Say a mystery word by saying one sound at a time. When all the sounds have been made, students are to blend the sounds together to tell the mystery word. Begin by providing an example so students know what is expected. For example, if the mystery word is *big*, say, /b/ pause /i/ pause /g/. Students should identify that the mystery word is *big*. If students have a difficult time, model saying the three sounds of the word again several times, each time with shorter pauses until the word sounds like normal speech.

As students demonstrate their understanding of the activity and their capability to blend, use mystery words with more sounds. For example, expand from words like *bat* to words such as *bend* and *bust*.

Use nonsense words as mystery words, too. Nonsense words are words that we do not use in the English language. An example of a nonsense word is *bip*. By using nonsense words, you can informally assess how well students understand the concept of blending.

The Same Sound (Phoneme Isolation)

List three words that begin with the same sound. Have students identify the sound they hear at the beginning of the words. For example, if you say *hen*, *hand*, and *hop*, students should indicate the beginning sound is /h/.

Alternatively, have the students identify the ending sound of three words. For example, if you say *sip*, *cop*, and *map*, students should indicate that they hear /p/ at the end of all three words.

Starts the Same (Phoneme Categorization)

Read a list of three words in succession, two of which begin with the same sound. Have students name the two words from the list that begin with the same sound. For example, have students listen for the /p/ sound. Say the words *pin*, *dog*, and *pat*. Students should indicate that the words *pin* and *pat* begin with the /p/ sound. Alternatively, the students may name the word that does not begin with /p/.

Target Sound (Phoneme Categorization)

Determine a list of words, about half of which begin with the targeted sound and half of which begin with other sounds. Say the words, one at a time. If the word begins with the targeted sound, students perform a prespecified activity or gesture. If the word does not begin with the sound, students do nothing. For example, if the target sound is /b/, students can buzz around the room when you say the word *baby*. If the word is *run*, students do nothing.

Best Practices: The Five Components of Reading (cont.)

Break It Down (Phoneme Segmentation)

Tell students you are going to say a word. They are to break the word apart or segment the word by saying each sound they hear, one sound at a time. For example, if you say the word *hat*, students should say /h/ pause /a/ pause /t/. Begin by modeling several examples for students.

Alliteration Sentences

Emphasize words that begin with the same sound by having students think of sentences in which all or most of the words begin with the same sound. For example, if students are learning about the /s/ sound, the following sentence could be made: *Sam sees a silly snake.* This activity can be done orally, or the sentence can be written down and students can illustrate a picture to correspond with the sentence.

First or Last (Phoneme Isolation)

Fold 3" x 5" index cards in half in order to create two 3" x 2.5" boxes. Draw a line on the fold to better differentiate the boxes. Provide each student with an index card and a manipulative such as a bear counter, a penny, or an eraser. Practice naming the sections of the card with students. For example, ask students to place their manipulative in the first box. Tell students that this is the beginning box because it is first. Ask students to place their manipulative in the second box. Tell students that this is the ending box because it is last. Be sure students understand the name and purpose of the two boxes before proceeding to the next step.

Determine the sound for which you want students to listen. Create a list of words, several of which have the determined sound at the beginning of the word, and several of which

have the sound at the end of the word. For example, if the sound you want students to listen for is /s/, use a list similar to the following:

Begins with /s/		Ends with /s/	
sit	soap	rice	cats
sag	salt	rocks	prince

Say a word from the list. If students hear /s/ at the beginning of the word, students should slide their manipulative onto the first or beginning box on the index card. If students hear /s/ at the end of the word, they should slide their manipulative onto the second or last box on the index card. If the word is *sad*, students should slide their manipulative into the first or beginning box because /s/ is at the beginning of the word. If the word is *pots*, students should slide their manipulative onto the ending or last box because /s/ is at the end of the word. Demonstrate and practice several examples with students until they understand what is expected.

Alternatively, make "First or Last" a movement activity by placing two pieces of paper on the floor in front of a student. Play the game in the same way. Say a word such as *sit*. If the student hears the /s/ sound at the beginning of the word, the student jumps or steps on the piece of paper that is on the left. If the word is *cats*, the student jumps or steps on the piece of paper on the right, because the /s/ sound is at the end of the word.

Introduction

Best Practices: The Five Components of Reading *(cont.)*

Rhyme Time

Say two words. If the words rhyme, students should perform one action. If the two words do not rhyme, students should perform another action. For example, say two words from the list below in succession. Have students indicate by smiling if the words rhyme. If the words do not rhyme, students should frown.

hot – dot   rhyme (smile)

ham – dog   do not rhyme (frown)

Once students demonstrate a good understanding of rhyming, an extension of the rhyming activity above is for the students to generate the two words. The teacher can then smile or frown in order to show if the words rhyme or do not rhyme. This is an excellent informal assessment. By monitoring the words the students provide, a combination of rhyming words and non-rhyming words, the teacher will be able to assess students' understanding.

Three Rhymes in a Row

Tell students you are going to say two words that rhyme. Students need to generate a third word that rhymes with the two you said. For example, if you say the words *pat* and *hat*, students might say the word *cat*. Repeat the three words in order to emphasize the rhyme.

They Rhyme

Read a list of three words in succession. The three words should include two words that rhyme and one word that does not rhyme. Students should determine which two words rhyme. For example, the teacher may say *cat*, *bet*, *mat*. Students should indicate that the words *cat* and *mat* rhyme.

Fluency

Fluency is the ability to read quickly and accurately while at the same time using good oral expression, proper phrasing, and appropriate pacing. Fluency is particularly important for young children who are just learning to read or struggling readers, or children learning English as a second language. These students expend too much cognitive energy decoding words letter by letter, thereby losing understanding of the material. Their attention and energy is focused on getting each sound correct rather than finding meaning and making sense of the text. This is clear when, after listening to a struggling reader, the student does not understand what has just been read. Children who read more fluently use their cognitive energy and attention to focus on the meaning of the print. They comprehend what they read. The fluent reader has enough attention in reserve to make connections between the text and their own background knowledge, which gives the reader a deeper understanding of the material. When oral reading of text is more fluent and sounds like natural speech, children are better able to pull from their own prior knowledge and background experiences for comprehension.

Building Comprehension

Good readers are taught to use a wide array of strategies to make sense of what they are reading. They are explicitly taught to make connections as they read by using their prior knowledge as well as their visualizing, inferring, and synthesizing skills.

Best Practices: The Five Components of Reading *(cont.)*

Good readers ask questions before they read, as they read, and after they read. Street signs, cereal boxes, and billboards all provide opportunities for readers to interact with words in a meaningful, purposeful way.

This book provides a variety of lessons and activities that will assist you with creative ideas for repeated readings for building fluency and developing comprehension. The lessons are designed to look beyond the color and context clues of environmental print to read words. A variety of writing activities and ways to reinforce making meaning during reading are provided, as well as ways to scaffold the development of comprehension strategies.

Building Vocabulary

Opportunities abound within the typical classroom for children to learn new vocabulary and to experiment with words. To learn new words, children must experience words in frequent, meaningful, and varied contexts. The more exposure a child has to words, the better able he or she is to read and comprehend. Vocabulary knowledge, then, is an important factor in reading comprehension.

Sight words are those high-frequency words that do not necessarily decode and that must be read with automaticity by children. The lessons in this book provide oral-reading opportunities for children of varying reading levels and different learning styles in a whole-class setting or in a small-group setting. The lessons and activities reinforce the sight words that children must recognize automatically. Sight words are repeated to develop visual memory and improve visual-auditory perception.

Vocabulary learning is comprised of roughly four stages: listening, speaking, reading, and writing. Children develop these components of vocabulary in this sequence as well. A child's first vocabulary is the listening vocabulary. Children arrive at school with a receptive vocabulary of thousands and thousands of words. Speaking vocabulary develops after the listening vocabulary. Reading and writing vocabulary begin expanding dramatically after the age of five or six. For very young children, the first words learned are those that are experienced within the home, family, and care-giving environments. As children interact with their environment, they construct and learn concepts for which words become labels. The environment for young children includes experiences with words on products, packaging, signs, and billboards.

Following basic principles for developing vocabulary with young children, the subsequent lesson plans address the following:

- teach useful words that young children will likely encounter.
- teach words that are conceptually related to others.
- teach words that relate to their background knowledge.
- generate an enthusiasm for and interest in words.

Introduction

Best Practices: Differentiation

Over the past few years, classrooms have evolved into diverse pools of learners. Gifted students, English language learners, learning-disabled students, high achievers, underachievers, and average students all come together to learn from one teacher. The teacher is expected to meet their diverse needs in one classroom. It brings back memories of the one-room schoolhouse from early American history. Not too long ago, lessons were designed to be one-size-fits-all. It was thought that students in the same grade level learned in similar ways. Today we know that viewpoint is faulty. Students have differing learning styles, come from different cultures, experience a variety of emotions, and have varied interests. For each subject, they also differ in academic readiness. At times, the challenges teachers face can be overwhelming. They struggle to figure out how to create learning environments that address the differences they find in their students.

What is differentiation? Carol Ann Tomlinson of the University of Virginia says, "Differentiation is simply a teacher attending to the learning needs of a particular student or small group of students, rather than teaching a class as though all individuals in it were basically alike" (2000). Differentiation can be accomplished by any teacher who keeps the learners at the forefront of his or her instruction. The effective teacher asks, "What am I going to do to shape instruction to meet the needs of all my learners?" One method or methodology will not reach all students.

Differentiation encompasses what is taught, how it is taught, and the products students create to show what they have learned. When differentiating curriculum, teachers become the organizers of learning opportunities within the classroom environment. These categories are often referred to as *content, process*, and *product*.

- **Content:** Differentiating the content means putting more depth into the curriculum by organizing the curriculum concepts and structure of knowledge.
- **Process:** Differentiating the process requires the use of varied instructional techniques and materials to enhance students' learning.
- **Product:** When products are differentiated, cognitive development and students' abilities to express themselves improves.

Why Should We Differentiate?

The more we understand how students learn, the more we understand why curriculum needs to be differentiated. Students make meaning out of what is taught in classrooms based on their prior understandings, learning styles, attitudes, and beliefs. Differentiated curriculum takes these into account. Research has shown that students need to be pushed just a little beyond their independence levels for real learning to take place (Csikszentmihalyi 1990). Differentiated curriculum provides an avenue by which lessons can challenge, but not overwhelm, students based on their ability levels. Both emotions and movement enhance the learning process and when students have the opportunity to study their interests, their motivation for learning increases (Piaget 1978). A differentiated classroom takes interests into account. Finally, we know that everyone learns in a variety of ways. Curriculum that is differentiated allows for a variety of grouping techniques and assignments so that teachers can reach students regardless of their backgrounds.

Best Practices:
Differentiation *(cont.)*

Teachers should differentiate content, process, and product according to students' characteristics. These characteristics include students' readiness, learning styles, and interests.

- **Readiness:** If a learning experience matches closely with students' previous skills and understanding of a topic, they will learn better.
- **Learning styles:** Teachers should create assignments that allow students to complete work according to their personal preferences and styles.
- **Interests:** If a topic sparks excitement in the students, then they will become involved in learning and better remember what is taught.

How to Begin Differentiating

As previously discussed, differentiation encompasses content, process, and product. Below are some specific ways in which teachers can differentiate within these three categories.

Teachers can differentiate content by:
- reading an excerpt of an article, as opposed to the entire article.
- reading shorter chunks of text over a longer period of time.

Teachers can differentiate process by:
- grouping students in different ways: whole class, teacher-directed groups, independent groups, partners, or individuals.
- providing scaffolds for students to be able to meet the expectations.
- breaking steps down into smaller parts to make each step more manageable.
- preteaching more difficult skills, vocabulary, or concepts prior to a whole-class lesson.

- having students read independently or with the teacher, depending on their reading level.

Teachers can differentiate product by allowing students to:

- create a photo collage versus a hand-drawn illustration.
- give an oral presentation versus a written presentation.
- choose a product that best fits their interests and strengths.

To make the activities within this book most effective, teachers should differentiate the lessons whenever possible. Not all students need to be engaged in exactly the same activity at the same time. The various activities included in this book provide opportunities for differentiating instruction within the lessons. Look for the heading "Time to Differentiate!" and the suggestions that are provided under this heading. You will find strategies for differentiating the lessons when preteaching each card as well as in each focus lesson. Strategies for differentiating instruction are given for above-level students, below-level students, and English learners. See the following page for specific stragies for supporting English language learners.

Introduction

Best Practices:
Differentiation *(cont.)*

English Language Support

Support for English language learners is crucial, as it gives them what they need to be successful in the classroom. Following are some effective research-based strategies that can be integrated into any lesson in this book:

- Draw from learners' background knowledge. Prime their knowledge, if necessary, using realia, photographs, visuals, field trips, guest speakers, etc.

- Provide an overview of the material, and allow students time to preview it.

- Explicitly point out text features, such as the title, headings, charts, graphs, photos, maps, boldfaced words, etc., and discuss how these help build comprehension.

- Lower the affective filter by providing a stress-free classroom environment, where students feel safe taking risks and trying to use more advanced vocabulary or sentence structures.

- During discussions, provide wait time to allow students to first process their thinking before accessing the language necessary to express it.

- Frequently check students' understanding of the material being presented.

- Speak at a slower pace.

- Provide language stems to scaffold students' oral and/or written responses. For example, when making predictions about a new piece of text, write on the board or chart paper, "I predict that _____" to give students the language model needed.

- Provide multiple opportunities for student interaction and discussion. According to Cummins (1981), children best learn the English language when they are actively involved in the process of communicating with one another.

- Model all desired behavior, including answering questions with a complete sentence, thinking aloud when reading or writing, maintaining eye contact with a speaker, using reference materials, asking for clarification, etc.

- Use graphic organizers to provide a visual representation and to facilitate prereading, postreading, and writing activities.

Correlation to Standards

The No Child Left Behind (NCLB) legislation mandates that all states adopt academic standards that identify the skills students will learn in kindergarten through grade twelve. While many states had already adopted academic standards prior to NCLB, the legislation set requirements to ensure the standards were detailed and comprehensive.

Standards are designed to focus instruction and guide adoption of curricula. Standards are statements that describe the criteria necessary for students to meet specific academic goals. They define the knowledge, skills, and content students should acquire at each level. Standards are also used to develop standardized tests to evaluate students' academic progress.

In many states today, teachers are required to demonstrate how their lessons meet state standards. State standards are used in the development of Shell Education products, so educators can be assured they meet the academic requirements of each state.

How to Find Your State Correlations

Shell Education is committed to producing educational materials that are research- and standards-based. In this effort, all products are correlated to the academic standards of all 50 states, the District of Columbia, and the Department of Defense Dependent Schools. You can print a correlation report customized for your state directly from our website at **http://www.shelleducation.com**. If you require assistance in printing correlation reports, please contact Customer Service at 1-877-777-3450.

McREL Compendium

Shell Education uses the Mid-continent Research for Education and Learning (McREL) compendium to create standards correlations. Each year, McREL analyzes state standards and revises the compendium. By following this procedure, they are able to produce a general compilation of national standards.

Each lesson in this book is based on McREL content standards. The following chart (pages 20–21) shows the McREL standards that correlate to each lesson used in the book. To see a state-specific correlation, visit the Shell Education website at **http://www.shelleducation.com**.

Introduction

Correlation to Standards

Standard	Benchmark	Lesson and Page Number
Standard 5 Uses the general skills and strategies of the reading process	**(K–2) 5.1** Uses mental images based on pictures and print to aid in comprehension of text	Unit 1 Lesson A (page 66) Unit 3 Lesson B (page 138)
	(K–2) 5.2 Uses meaning clues (e.g., picture captions, title, cover, headings, story structure, story topic) to aid comprehension and make predictions about content (e.g., action, events, character's behavior)	Unit 2 Lesson A (page 106)
	(Pre-K) 5.8 Knows that print appears in different forms (e.g., labels, letters, storybooks) and serves different purposes (e.g., to inform)	Unit 2 Lessons A and B (pages 106 and 112) Unit 4 Lesson B (page 162)
	(Pre-K) 5.13 Uses visual and verbal cues, including pictures, to comprehend new words and stories	Unit 1 Lesson A (page 66)
Standard 6 Uses reading skills and strategies to understand and interpret a variety of literary texts	**(Pre-K) 6.1** Knows the sequence of events (e.g., beginning, middle, and end) in a story	Unit 1 Lesson B (page 72) Unit 3 Lesson A (page 132)

Correlation to Standards *(cont.)*

Standard	Benchmark	Lesson and Page Number
Standard 6 Uses reading skills and strategies to understand and interpret a variety of literary texts	(K–2) 6.2 Knows the basic characteristics of familiar genres (e.g., picture books, fairy tales, nursery rhymes)	Unit 2 Lesson B (page 112)
	(K–2) 6.3 Knows setting, main characters, main events, sequence, and problems in stories	Unit 1 Lesson B (page 72)
	(Pre-K) Standard 6.5 Relates stories to his/her own life and experience	Unit 3 Lesson B (page 138) Unit 4 Lesson A (page 156)
	(K–2) 6.5 Relates stories to personal experiences (e.g., events, characters, conflicts, themes)	Unit 4 Lesson A (page 156)
Standard 7 Uses reading skills and strategies to understand and interpret a variety of informational texts	(K–2) 7.1 Uses reading skills and strategies to understand a variety of informational texts (e.g., written directions, signs, captions, warning labels, informational books)	Unit 3 Lesson A (page 132) Unit 4 Lesson B (page 162)

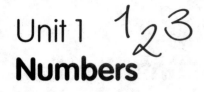

Numbers

Operations

Sort and Classify

Time and Money

Introduction to Unit 1: Numbers

This unit introduces students to the numbers 1–20. Students will learn to recognize chronological, logical, and sequential order. In this unit, students will also learn to use visualization strategies to comprehend text.

Skills Taught in This Unit

- observing different aspects of a text
- sharing observations orally
- understanding the connection between amounts and written numbers
- understanding number sentences
- visualizing information
- filling in missing information
- predicting information
- understanding the importance of order in texts
- recognizing chronological, logical, or sequential order
- reviewing numbers 1–20
- writing numbers 1–20

Directions for the Teacher

You have many different options when teaching this unit. You can use the nonfiction cards and teach the content using the strategies that precede each card. Or, you can teach nonfiction skills and strategies by teaching the whole unit, starting with the introductory lesson, then teaching the focus lesson, and then following up with the center activities. This format repeats for the second lesson in the unit. Conclude the unit by teaching the wrap-up activity to tie all the nonfiction text and skills together.

Activating Prior Knowledge

Share Math Card 1 with students. Ask them to look at the picture closely and describe what they see. Ask students to look at the pictured object. Ask students to help you count the objects they see in the picture. Tell them that the number on the card is a number 1 and talk about this number. Tell them that there is one item in the picture and it is a train. Ask students to hold up one finger. Tell students that you would like them to learn how to make a number 1. Model on the board or on a sheet of chart paper how to make a number 1. Tell them to start at the top and draw a straight line down. Ask students to practice making the number 1 in the air with their pointer fingers. Give students an opportunity to practice making the number 1 by providing a number-making center in the classroom. For example, have them practice making the number 1 in salt.

Language Development

Ask students to sit in a circle near you. Direct students' attention to the number 1 at the top of the card. Ask them to make a number 1 in the air using their pointer fingers. Talk with students about how there is only one way to make one and that it is a special number. Ask students to think of things that only come in ones. For example, we have one head and one body, and there is only one of each of us. Ask students to quietly get one object from somewhere in the classroom and bring it back to share with the group. Model this for students before you send them out on their own. When students are back with the group and they have their one object, give each one a chance to tell about the object he or she chose. To conclude, put one object in the middle of your circle, talk about the number 1, and ask students to practice making the number 1 in the air.

Building Knowledge and Comprehension

Before this activity, print on the bottom of a large sheet of construction paper the phrase, "There is only one _____." Make and distribute a copy for each student. Share Math Card 1 with students and ask them to make a number 1 in the air with their pointer fingers. Ask students to draw a picture of themselves in the middle of the page. Direct their attention to the sentence at the bottom of the construction paper. Ask students to point to the words while you read the sentence to them. Ask students to read the sentence with you. Tell them to write their names in the blank at the end of the sentence. Talk about how they are unique and special and that there is only one of them. If using Math Cards 1–20, save each student's "one" page in a folder so that he or she can make a book of the numbers 1–20.

Time to Differentiate!

For English language learners, build their vocabulary for the Activating Prior Knowledge lesson. Point to and name the object on the card. Provide some describing words. If possible, bring in some wooden trains for students to look at and touch.

For below-level students, scaffold the Activating Prior Knowledge lesson by providing a model for students to follow as they practice making the number 1. For example, use a highlighter to write the number on chart paper and then ask students to trace the number in pencil.

PHOTO CREDIT: © 2002 PHOTODISC

1
one

Unit 1
Numbers

1 2 3

two

Activating Prior Knowledge

Share Math Card 2 with students. Ask them to look at the picture closely and describe what they see. Ask students to look at the pictured objects. Talk with students about where a person could find the pictured objects. Tell them that the number on the card is a number 2 and talk about this number. Tell them that there are two items in the picture and that they are pineapples. Ask students to hold up two fingers. Ask students to look around the room so they can see what two fingers look like. Tell students that you would like them to learn how to make a number 2. Model on the board or on a sheet of chart paper how to make a number 2. Ask students to practice making the number 2 in the air with their pointer fingers. Give students an opportunity to practice making the number 2 by providing a number-making center in the classroom. For example, have them practice making the number 2 out of clay.

Language Development

Ask students to sit in a circle near you. Direct students' attention to the number 2 at the top of the card. Ask them to make a number 2 in the air using their pointer fingers. Talk with students about the different ways to make two. Ask students to think of things that only come in twos. For example, we have two arms, two legs, two hands, and two feet. Ask students to quietly get two objects from somewhere in the classroom and bring them back to share with the group. Model first how to choose two objects. When students are back with the group, give each one a chance to tell about the objects he or she chose. To conclude, put two objects in the middle of your circle, talk about the number 2, and ask them to practice making the number 2 in the air.

Building Knowledge and Comprehension

Print on the bottom of a large sheet of construction paper the phrase, "There are two _____." Make and distribute a copy for each student. Share Math Card 2 with students and ask them to make a number 2 in the air with their pointer fingers. Give each student a magazine. Tell students to look in the magazine and cut out things in twos. Ask students to glue the pictures to the construction paper. Direct their attention to the sentence at the bottom of the construction paper. Ask students to point to the words while you read the sentence to them. Help them write the names of the objects they cut out in the blank at the end of the sentence. If using Math Cards 1–20, save each student's "two" page in a folder so that he or she can make a book of the numbers 1–20.

Time to Differentiate!

For English language learners, label with card with English words before you begin the lesson. Then point to and read each word before asking students to repeat it. Continue to add relevant words as you discuss the card and activate prior knowledge.

For below-level students, review the number 2 and show students several examples of that quantity. Show students how to point to and count the objects on the card. Then invite each student to point to and count the objects with you.

PHOTO CREDIT: © 2002 PHOTODISC

2
two

Unit 1  Numbers

three

Activating Prior Knowledge

Share Math Card 3 with students. Ask them to look at the picture closely and describe what they see. Ask students to look at the pictured objects. Ask students to help you count the objects pictured. Tell them that the number on the card is a number 3 and talk about what makes three. Tell them that there are three dogs in the picture. Ask students to hold up three fingers. Tell students that you would like them to learn how to make a number 3. Model on the board or on a sheet of chart paper how to make a number 3. Ask students to practice making the number 3 in the air with their pointer fingers. Give students an opportunity to practice making the number 3 by providing a number-making center in the classroom. For example, have them practice making the number 3 from a rubbing of sand paper.

Language Development

Ask students to sit in a circle near you. Direct students' attention to the number 3 at the top of the card. Ask them to make a number 3 in the air using their pointer fingers. Talk with students about how to make three. Ask students to think of things that only come in threes. For example, triplets are three people born to the same mother at the same time. Ask students to quietly get three objects from somewhere in the classroom and bring the objects back to share with the group. Model for students how to choose three objects. When students are back with the group and they have their three objects, give each one a chance to tell about the objects he or she chose. To conclude, put three objects in the middle of your circle, talk about the number 3, and ask students to practice making the number 3 in the air.

Building Knowledge and Comprehension

Before this activity, print on the bottom of a large sheet of construction paper the phrase, "There are three _____." Make and distribute a copy for each student. Share Math Card 3 with students and ask them to make a number 3 in the air with their pointer fingers. Give each student a magazine. Tell students to look in the magazine and cut out three pictures of one object. Ask students to glue the pictures to the construction paper. Direct their attention to the sentence at the bottom of the page. Ask students to read the sentence with you. Help them write the name of the objects they cut out in the blank at the end of the sentence. Read any books you may have that show objects in threes. If using Math Cards 1–20, save each student's "three" page in a folder so that he or she can make a book of the numbers 1–20. Keep the books in a class library for students to read.

Time to Differentiate!

For English language learners, label with card with English words before you begin the lesson. Then point to and read each word before asking students to repeat it. Continue to add relevant words as you discuss the card and activate prior knowledge.

For below-level students, review the number 3 and show students several examples of that quantity. Show students how to point to and count the objects on the card. Then invite each student to point to and count the objects with you.

PHOTO CREDIT: © 2002 PHOTODISC

3
three

Activating Prior Knowledge

Show students Math Card 4. Ask them to look closely and describe what they see in the picture. Ask students to help you count the objects pictured. Tell them that the number on the card is a number 4 and talk about what makes four. Tell them that there are four strawberries in the picture. Ask students to hold up four fingers. Ask students to look around the room so they can see what four fingers look like. Tell students that you would like them to learn how to make a number 4. Model on the board or on a sheet of chart paper how to make a number 4. Ask students to practice making the number 4 in the air with their pointer fingers. Give students an opportunity to practice making the number 4 by providing a number-making center in the classroom. For example, have them practice making the number 4 with counting cubes.

Language Development

Ask students to sit in a circle near you. Direct students' attention to the number 4 at the top of the card. Ask them to make a number 4 in the air using their pointer fingers. Talk with students about how to make four. Ask students to think of things that only come in fours. For example, there are four tires on a car. Ask students to quietly get four objects from somewhere in the classroom and bring the objects back to share with the group. Model for students how to choose four objects. When students are back with the group and they have their four objects, give each one a chance to tell about the objects he or she chose. To conclude, put four objects in the middle of your circle, talk about the number 4, and ask students to practice making the number 4 in the air.

Building Knowledge and Comprehension

Prior to this activity, take pictures of students in groups of four. Make and distribute a copy of the picture for each student to use. Print on the bottom of a large sheet of construction paper the sentences, "There are four students. Their names are _____." Make a copy for each student. Share Math Card 4 with students and ask them to make a number 4 in the air with their pointer fingers. Give each student his or her picture. Ask students to glue the picture in the middle of the page. Direct their attention to the sentences at the bottom of the construction paper. Ask students to point to the words while you read the sentences to them. Help them write the names of the students pictured in the blank at the end of the second sentence. If using Math Cards 1–20, save each student's "four" page in a folder so that he or she can make a book of the numbers 1–20.

Time to Differentiate!

For English language learners, scaffold the Language Development lesson by providing oral models for the discussion. Model how to tell about the objects you chose from the room. Then prompt students to follow your model. For example, say, "I have four yellow pencils. I picked them from the math center." Then guide students in using your model.

For below-level students, scaffold the Language Development lesson. Provide students with two groups of objects—one with the correct quantity and one with an incorrect quantity. Help students count each group of objects and identify which group matches the number for this lesson. Then discuss the objects as a group.

PHOTO CREDIT: PHOTODISC

4
four

Activating Prior Knowledge

Show Math Card 5 to students. Ask them to look at the picture and describe what they see. Ask students to count the teddy bears as you point to them. Tell them that the number on the card is a number 5. Ask students to hold up five fingers. Ask students to look around the room so they can see what five fingers look like. Tell students that you would like them to learn how to make a number 5. Model on the board or on a sheet of chart paper how to make a number 5. Ask students to practice making the number 5 in the air with their pointer fingers. Give students an opportunity to practice making the number 5 by providing a number-making center in the classroom. For example, have students practice making the number 5 by gluing beans on construction paper.

Language Development

Ask students to sit in a circle near you. Direct students' attention to the number 5 at the top of the card. Ask them to make a number 5 in the air using their pointer fingers. Talk with students about how to make five. Ask students to think of things that only come in fives. For example, we have five fingers on each hand and five toes on each foot. Ask students to quietly get five objects from somewhere in the classroom and bring the objects back to share with the group. Model for students how to choose five objects. When students are back with the group and they have their five objects, give each one a chance to tell about the objects he or she chose. To conclude, put five objects in the middle of your circle, talk about the number 5, and ask students to practice making the number 5 in the air.

Building Knowledge and Comprehension

Print on the bottom of a large sheet of construction paper the phrase, "There are five _____." Make and distribute a copy for each student. Share Math Card 5 with students and ask them to make a number five in the air with their pointer fingers. Give each student a magazine. Tell students to look in the magazine and cut out five things that are the same. Ask students to glue the pictures to the construction paper. Direct their attention to the sentence at the bottom of the construction paper. Ask students to point to the words while you read the sentence to them. Ask students to read the sentence with you. Help them write the names of the objects they cut out in the blank at the end of the sentence. If using Math Cards 1–20, save each student's "five" page in a folder so that he or she can make a book of the numbers 1–20.

Time to Differentiate!

For English language learners, provide extra assistance to help students complete the Building Knowledge and Comprehension activity. Draw a picture of each step on the board. Then talk students through each step as you point to the drawing on the board.

For below-level students, provide them with a model of the number 5 to refer to during these lessons. For example, write the number 5 on a sheet of paper and give one copy to each student. As you lead students through the lessons, encourage students to trace the number with their pointer fingers before making the number in the air.

PHOTO CREDIT: © 2002 PHOTODISC

5
five

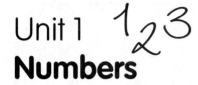
Activating Prior Knowledge

Show students Math Card 6. Ask them to look closely at the picture and describe what they see. Talk with students about where a person could find the pictured objects. Tell them that the number on the card is a number 6 and talk about the number. Tell them that there are six items in the picture and they are pigs. Ask students to hold up six fingers. Ask students to look around the room so they can see what six fingers look like. Tell students that you would like them to learn how to make a number 6. Model on the board or on a sheet of chart paper how to make a number 6. Ask students to practice making the number 6 in the air with their pointer fingers. Give students an opportunity to practice making the number 6 by providing a number-making center in the classroom. For example, have students practice making the number 6 out of counting tiles.

Language Development

Ask students to sit in a circle near you. Direct their attention to the number 6 at the top of the card. Ask them to make a number 6 in the air using their pointer fingers. Talk with students about the different ways to make six. Use language like, "two and four make six," or, "three and three make six." Explain to students that six is half of a dozen. If possible, bring in a half-dozen carton of eggs to show students. Compare the half dozen eggs to a dozen eggs. Ask students to quietly get six objects from somewhere in the classroom and bring them back to share with the group. Model first how to choose six objects. When students are back with the group, give each one a chance to tell about the objects he or she chose. To conclude, put six objects in the middle of your circle, talk about the number 6, and ask students to practice making the number 6 in the air.

Building Knowledge and Comprehension

Before this activity, print on the bottom of a large sheet of construction paper the phrase, "There are six _____." Make and distribute a copy for each student. Share Math Card 6 with students and ask them to make a number 6 in the air with their pointer fingers. Ask students to return to their workspace and draw six objects on their papers. Tell them that the objects that they draw must be similar, for example, six dogs or six books. Direct their attention to the sentence at the bottom of the construction paper. Ask students to point to the words while you read the sentence to them. Ask students to read the sentence with you. Help them write the names of the objects they drew in the blank at the end of the sentence. If using Math Cards 1–20, save each student's "six" page in a folder so that he or she can make a book of the numbers 1–20. Keep the completed books in a class library for students to read.

Time to Differentiate!

For English language learners, build their vocabulary for the Activating Prior Knowledge lesson. Point to and name the objects on the card. Provide some describing words. If possible, bring in some plastic toy pigs for students to look at and discuss.

For below-level students, scaffold the Activating Prior Knowledge lesson by providing a model for students to follow as they practice making the number 6. For example, use a highlighter to write the number on chart paper and then ask students to trace the number in pencil.

PHOTO CREDIT: © 2002 PHOTODISC

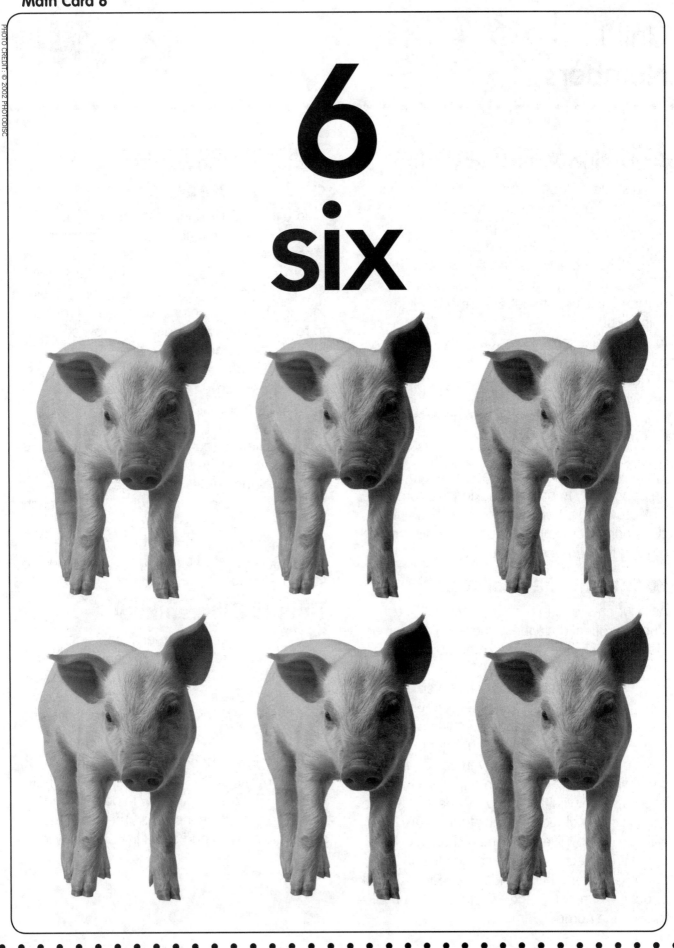

seven

Activating Prior Knowledge

Show students Math Card 7. Ask them to look closely at the picture and describe what they see. Ask students to look at the pictured objects. Talk with students about where a person could find the pictured objects. Tell them that the number on the card is a number 7 and talk about the number. Tell them that there are seven items in the picture and they are pears. Ask students to count the objects while you point to them. Ask students to hold up seven fingers. Ask students to look around the room so they can see what seven fingers look like. Tell students that you would like them to learn how to make a number 7. Model how to make a number 7. Ask students to practice making the number 7 in the air with their pointer fingers. Give students an opportunity to practice making the number 7 by providing a number-making center in the classroom. For example, have students practice making the number 7 with paint.

Language Development

Ask students to sit in a circle near you. Direct students' attention to the number 7 at the top of the card. Ask them to make a number 7 in the air using their pointer fingers. Talk with students about the different ways to make seven. Using counting cubes, model for students how to make seven. Use language like, "two and five make seven," or, "three plus four equals seven." Ask students to quietly get seven objects from somewhere in the classroom and bring them back to share with the group. Model first how to choose seven objects. When students are back with the group, give each one a chance to tell about the objects he or she chose. To conclude, put seven objects in the middle of your circle, talk about the number 7, and ask students to practice making the number 7 in the air.

Building Knowledge and Comprehension

Before this activity, print on the bottom of a large sheet of construction paper the phrase, "There are seven _____." Make and distribute a copy for each student. Share Math Card 7 with students and ask them to make a number 7 in the air with their pointer fingers. Ask students to return to their workspace and draw seven objects on their papers. Tell them that the objects they draw must be similar, for example, seven stars or seven flowers. Direct their attention to the sentence at the bottom of the construction paper. Ask students to point to the words while you read the sentence to them. Ask students to read the sentence with you. Help them write the names of the objects they drew in the blank. If using Math Cards 1–20, save each student's "seven" page in a folder so that he or she can make a book of the numbers 1–20. Keep the completed books in a class library for students to read.

Time to Differentiate!

For English language learners, label each card with English words before you begin the lesson. Then point to and read each word before asking students to repeat it. Continue to add relevant words as you discuss the card and activate prior knowledge.

For below-level students, review the number 7 and show students several examples of that quantity. Show students how to point to and count the objects on the card. Then invite each student to point to and count the objects with you.

PHOTO CREDIT: © 2002 PHOTODISC

7
seven

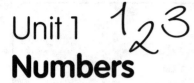
Activating Prior Knowledge

Show students Math Card 8. Ask them to look closely at the picture and describe what they see. Talk with students about where a person could find the pictured objects. Tell them that the number on the card is a number 8 and talk about the number. Tell them that there are eight items in the picture and that they are chicks. Have students count the chicks while you point to them. Ask students to hold up eight fingers. Ask students to look around the room so they can see what eight fingers look like. Tell students that you would like them to learn how to make a number 8. Model how to write a number 8. Ask students to practice making the number 8 in the air with their pointer fingers. Give students an opportunity to practice making the number 8 by providing a number-making center in the classroom. For example, have students practice making the number 8 in liquid soap.

Language Development

Ask students to sit in a circle near you. Direct students' attention to the number 8 at the top of the card. Ask them to make a number 8 in the air using their pointer fingers. Talk about how to spell *eight* and what letter it begins with. Talk with students about the different ways to make eight. Using a manipulative like color tiles, model for students different ways to make eight. Use language like, "two and six make eight," or, "three plus five equals eight." Ask students to quietly get eight objects from somewhere in the classroom and bring them back to share with the group. Model first how to choose eight objects. Give each student a chance to tell about the objects he or she chose. To conclude, put eight objects in the middle of your circle, talk about the number 8, and ask students to practice making the number 8 in the air.

Building Knowledge and Comprehension

Before this activity, print on the bottom of a large sheet of construction paper the phrase, "There are eight _____." Make and distribute a copy for each student. Share Math Card 8 with students and ask them to make a number 8 in the air with their pointer fingers. Give each student a magazine. Tell students to look in the magazine and cut out eight things that are the same. Ask students to glue the pictures to the construction paper. Direct their attention to the sentence at the bottom of the construction paper. Ask students to point to the words while you read the sentence to them. Help them write the names of the objects they cut out in the blank at the end of the sentence. If using Math Cards 1–20, save each student's "eight" page in a folder so that he or she can make a book of the numbers 1–20. Keep the completed books in a class library for students to read.

Time to Differentiate!

For English language learners, scaffold the Building Knowledge and Comprehension lesson by helping them label their cut-out pictures. Show students how we use the plural noun to show "more than one." Encourage students to use the correct word when they write their sentences.

For below-level students, scaffold the Building Knowledge and Comprehension lesson. Provide students with the correct number of objects cut out from a magazine. Work with students in a small group to practice counting the objects correctly.

PHOTO CREDIT: EYEWIRE

8
eight

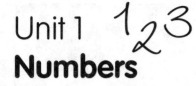
Activating Prior Knowledge

Show students Math Card 9. Ask them to look at the picture and describe what they see. Talk with students about where a person could find the pictured objects. Tell them that the number on the card is a number 9 and talk about the number. Tell them that there are nine items in the picture and that they are butterflies. Have students count the butterflies while you point to them. Ask students to hold up nine fingers. Ask students to look around the room so they can see what nine fingers look like. Tell students that you would like them to learn how to make a number 9. Model how to write a number 9. Ask students to practice making the number 9 in the air with their pointer fingers. Give students an opportunity to practice making the number 9 by providing a number-making center in the classroom. For example, have students practice making the number 9 in shaving cream.

Language Development

Ask students to sit in a circle near you. Direct students' attention to the number 9 at the top of the card. Ask them to make a number 9 in the air using their pointer fingers. Talk about how to spell *nine* and what letter it begins with. Talk with students about the different ways to make nine. Using a manipulative, model for students different ways to make nine. Use language like, "two and seven make nine," or, "four plus five equals nine." Ask students to quietly get nine objects from somewhere in the classroom and bring them back to share with the group. Model this first. Give each student a chance to tell about the objects he or she chose. To conclude, put nine objects in the middle of your circle, talk about the number 9, and ask students to practice making the number 9 in the air.

Building Knowledge and Comprehension

Before this activity, print on the bottom of a large sheet of construction paper the phrase, "There are nine _____." Make and distribute a copy for each student. Share Math Card 9 with students and ask them to make a number 9 in the air with their pointer fingers. Give each student stickers. Tell students to arrange nine stickers on the construction paper. Direct their attention to the sentence at the bottom of the construction paper. Ask students to point to the words while you read the sentence to them. Ask students to read the sentence with you. Help them write the names of the objects they cut out in the blank at the end of the sentence. If using Math Cards 1–20, save each student's "nine" page in a folder so that he or she can make a book of the numbers 1–20. Keep the completed books in a class library for students to read.

Time to Differentiate!

For English language learners, scaffold the Language Development lesson by providing oral models for the discussion. Model how to tell about the objects you chose from the room. Then prompt students to follow your model. For example, say, "I have nine yellow pencils. I picked them from the math center." Then guide students in using your model.

For below-level students, scaffold the Language Development lesson. Provide students with two groups of objects—one with the correct quantity and one with an incorrect quantity. Help students count each group of objects and identify which group matches the number for this lesson. Then discuss the objects as a group.

PHOTO CREDIT: © 2002 PHOTODISC

9
nine

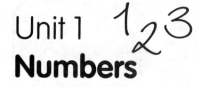
Activating Prior Knowledge

Show students Math Card 10. Ask them to look at the picture and describe what they see. Talk with students about where a person could find the pictured objects. Tell them that the number on the card is a number 10 and talk about the number. Tell them that there are 10 items in the picture and that they are toy soldiers. Have students count the toy soldiers while you point to them. Ask students to hold up 10 fingers. Ask students to look around the room to see what 10 fingers look like. Tell students that you would like them to learn how to make a number 10. Model how to write a number 10. Ask students to practice making the number 10 in the air with their pointer fingers. Give students an opportunity to practice making the number 10 by providing a number-making center in the classroom. For example, have students practice making the number 10 out of yarn.

Language Development

Ask students to sit in a circle near you. Direct students' attention to the number 10 at the top of the card. Ask them to make a number 10 in the air using their pointer fingers. Talk about how to spell *ten* and what letter it begins with. Talk with students about the different ways to make 10. Using a manipulative like color tiles, model for students different ways to make 10. Use language like, "four and six make ten," or, "five plus five equals ten." Ask students to quietly get 10 objects from somewhere in the classroom and bring them back to share with the group. Model first how to choose 10 objects. Give each student a chance to tell about the objects he or she chose. To conclude, put 10 objects in the middle of your circle, talk about the number 10, and ask students to practice making the number 10 in the air.

Building Knowledge and Comprehension

Before this activity, print at the top of a large sheet of construction paper the phrase, "There are ten _____." Print at the bottom of the paper, "_____ rhymes with ten." Make and distribute a copy for each student. Share Math Card 10 with students. Direct students' attention to the two sentences on the paper. Ask students to read the sentences. Help them write a word that rhymes with *ten*. Then have students draw 10 of that object. If using Math Cards 1–20, save each student's "ten" page in a folder so that he or she can make a book of the numbers 1–20. Keep the completed books in a class library for students to read.

Time to Differentiate!

For English language learners, provide extra assistance to help students complete the Building Knowledge and Comprehension activity. Draw a picture of each step on the board. Then talk students through each step as you point to the drawing on the board.

For below-level students, provide them with a model of the number 10 to refer to during these lessons. For example, write the number 10 on a sheet of paper and give one copy to each student. As you lead students through the lessons, encourage students to trace the number with their pointer fingers before making the number in the air.

PHOTO CREDIT: © 2002 PHOTODISC

10
ten

Unit 1
Numbers 1₂3

eleven

Activating Prior Knowledge

Show students Math Card 11. Ask them to look closely at the picture and describe what they see. Talk with students about where a person could find the pictured objects. Tell them that the number on the card is a number 11 and talk about the number. Tell them that there are 11 items in the picture and that they are shovels and pails. Have students count the pails while you point to them. Tell students that you would like them to learn how to make a number 11. Model how to write a number 11. Ask students to practice making the number 11 in the air with their pointer fingers. Give students an opportunity to practice making the number 11 by providing a number-making center in the classroom. For example, have students practice making the number 11 with clay.

Language Development

Ask students to sit in a circle near you. Direct their attention to the number 11 at the top of the card. Ask them to make a number 11 in the air using their pointer fingers. Talk about how to spell *eleven* and what letter it begins with. Talk with students about the different ways to make 11. Using counting cubes, model for students different ways to make 11. Use language like, "ten and one make eleven," or, "three plus eight equals eleven." Talk about the number problem that is written on the card. Ask students to quietly get 11 objects from the classroom and bring them back to the group. Model first how to choose 11 objects. Give each student a chance to tell about the objects he or she chose. To conclude, put 11 objects in the middle of your circle, talk about the number 11, and ask students to practice making the number 11 in the air.

Building Knowledge and Comprehension

Before this activity, print on the bottom of a large sheet of construction paper the phrase, "There are eleven _____." Make and distribute a copy for each student. Share Math Card 11 with students and ask them to make a number 11 in the air with their pointer fingers. Give each student a magazine. Tell students to look in the magazine and cut out 11 of the same thing. Ask students to glue the pictures to the construction paper. Direct their attention to the sentence at the bottom of the construction paper. Ask students to point to the words while you read the sentence to them. Help them write the name of the objects they cut out in the blank at the end of the sentence. If using Math Cards 1–20, save each student's "eleven" page in a folder so that he or she can make a book of the numbers 1–20. Keep the completed books in a class library for students to read.

Time to Differentiate!

For English language learners, build their vocabulary for the Activating Prior Knowledge lesson. Point to and name the objects on the card. Provide some describing words. If possible, bring in some shovels and buckets for students to look at and feel.

For below-level students, scaffold the Activating Prior Knowledge lesson by providing a model for students to follow as they practice making the number 11. For example, use a highlighter to write the number on chart paper and then ask students to trace the number in pencil.

PHOTO CREDIT: © 2002 PHOTODISC

11
eleven

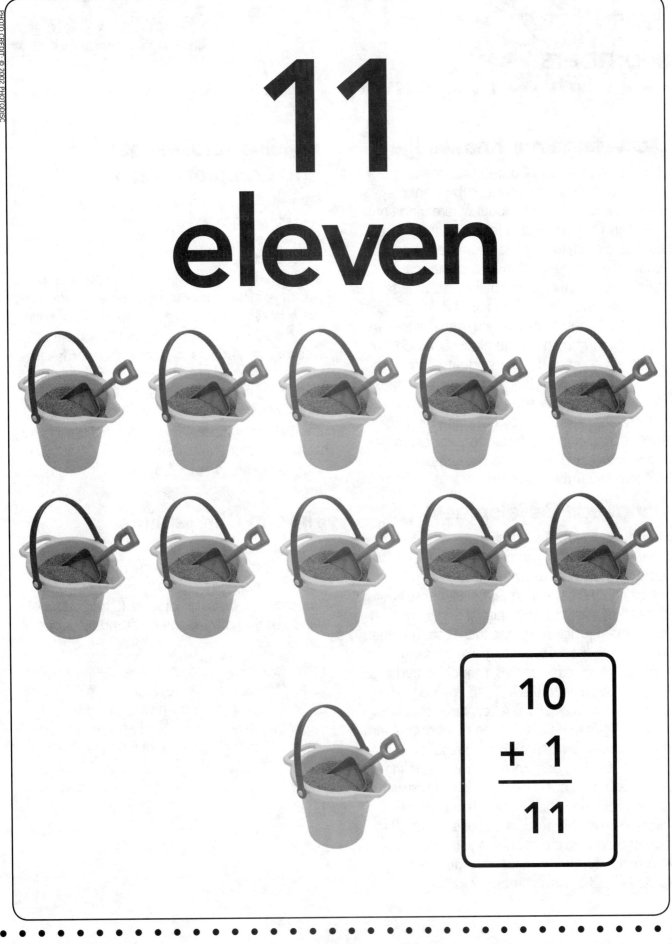

$$\begin{array}{r} 10 \\ +\ 1 \\ \hline 11 \end{array}$$

Activating Prior Knowledge

Show students Math Card 12. Ask them to look closely at the picture and describe what they see. Talk with students about where a person could find the pictured objects. Tell them that the number on the card is a number 12 and talk about the number. Tell them that there are 12 items in the picture and that they are starfish. Have students count the starfish while you point to them. Tell students that you would like them to learn how to make a number 12. Model how to write a number 12. Ask students to practice making the number 12 in the air with their pointer fingers. Give students an opportunity to practice making the number 12 by providing a number-making center in the classroom. For example, have them practice making the number 12 with chenille sticks (pipe cleaners).

Language Development

Ask students to sit in a circle near you. Direct their attention to the number 12 at the top of the card. Ask them to make a number 12 in the air using their pointer fingers. Talk about how to spell *twelve* and what letter it begins with. Have them practice making the /t/ sound. Talk about the different ways to make 12. Using manipulatives such as tiles, model for students different ways to make 12. Use language like, "ten and two make twelve," or "three plus nine equals twelve." Talk about the number problem that is written on the card. Ask students to quietly get 12 objects from somewhere in the classroom and bring them back to share with the group. Give each student a chance to share about the objects he or she chose. To conclude, put 12 objects in the middle of your circle, talk about the number 12, and ask students to practice making the number 12 in the air.

Building Knowledge and Comprehension

Before this activity, print on the bottom of a large sheet of construction paper the phrase, "There are twelve _____." Make and distribute a copy for each student. Share Math Card 12 with students and ask them to make a number 12 in the air with their pointer fingers. Tell students to draw 12 of the same thing. Direct their attention to the sentence at the bottom of the construction paper. Ask students to point to the words while you read the sentence to them. Ask students to read the sentence with you. Help them write the name of the objects they drew in the blank at the end of the sentence. If using Math Cards 1–20, save each student's "twelve" page in a folder so that he or she can make a book of the numbers 1–20.

Time to Differentiate!

For English language learners, label with card with English words before you begin the lesson. Then point to and read each word before asking students to repeat it. Continue to add relevant words as you discuss the card and activate prior knowledge.

For below-level students, review the number 12 and show students several examples of that quantity. Show students how to point to and count the objects on the card. Then invite each student to point to and count the objects with you.

PHOTO CREDIT: © 2002 PHOTODISC

12
twelve

$$\begin{array}{r} 10 \\ +\ 2 \\ \hline 12 \end{array}$$

Unit 1 123
Numbers

thirteen

Activating Prior Knowledge

Show students Math Card 13. Ask them to look closely at the picture and describe what they see. Talk with students about where a person could find the pictured objects and what they are used for. Tell them that the number on the card is a number 13 and talk about the number. Tell them that there are 13 soccer balls in the picture. Have students count the balls while you point to them. Tell students that you would like them to learn how to make a number 13. Model how to write a number 13. Ask students to practice making the number 13 in the air with their pointer fingers. Give students an opportunity to practice making the number 13 by providing a number-making center in the classroom. For example, have students practice making the number 13 in sand.

Language Development

Ask students to sit in a circle near you. Direct their attention to the number 13 at the top of the card. Ask them to make a number 13 in the air using their pointer fingers. Talk about how to spell *thirteen* and have students practice saying the /th/ digraph. Talk about the different ways to make 13. Using a manipulative like color tiles, model for students different ways to make 13. Use language like, "ten and three make thirteen," or "five plus eight equals thirteen." Talk about the number problem that is written on the card. Ask students to quietly get 13 objects in the classroom and bring them back to the group. Give each one a chance to tell about the objects he or she chose. To conclude, put 13 objects in the middle of your circle, talk about the number 13, and ask students to practice making the number 13 in the air.

Building Knowledge and Comprehension

Print a blank number sentence at the bottom of a sheet of paper "_____+_____=_____." Make and distribute a copy of the page for each student. Share Math Card 13 with students and ask them to make a number 13 in the air with their pointer fingers. Tell students to think about their favorite sport and the equipment used to play that sport. Give each student two different kinds of sports stickers or stamps. Ask students to add 13 stickers or stamps to the paper, using some of each kind (for example: 10 baseball bats and three footballs). Direct their attention to the number sentence on the page. Tell them to fill in the number sentence at the bottom to show how many stickers or stamps of each kind were used. Ask students to point to the numbers while you read the number sentence to them. If using Math Cards 1–20, save each student's "thirteen" page in a folder so that he or she can make a book of the numbers 1–20. Keep the completed books in a class library for students to read.

Time to Differentiate!

For English language learners, scaffold the Building Knowledge and Comprehension lesson by helping them label their number sentence pictures. Show students how we use the plural noun to show "more than one." Encourage students to use the correct word when they write their sentences.

For below-level students, scaffold the Building Knowledge and Comprehension lesson. Work with students in a small group to practice counting the objects correctly.

13
thirteen

$$\begin{array}{r} 10 \\ +\ 3 \\ \hline 13 \end{array}$$

PHOTO CREDIT: © 2002 PHOTODISC

fourteen

Activating Prior Knowledge

Show students Math Card 14. Ask them to look closely at the picture and describe what they see. Talk with students about where a person could find a flag and why it is significant. Tell them that the number on the card is a number 14 and talk about the number. Tell them that there are 14 flags in the picture. Have students count the flags while you point to them. Tell students that you would like them to learn how to make a number 14. Model on the board or on a sheet of chart paper how to write a number 14. Ask students to practice making the number 14 in the air with their pointer fingers. Give students an opportunity to practice making the number 14 by providing a number-making center in the classroom. For example, have students practice making the number 14 with beads.

Language Development

Ask students to sit in a circle near you. Direct their attention to the number 14 at the top of the card. Ask them to make a number 14 in the air using their pointer fingers. Talk about how to spell *fourteen* and have students practice making the /f/ sound. Talk with students about the different ways to make 14. Using counting cubes, model different ways to make 14. Use language like, "ten and four make fourteen," or, "five plus nine equals fourteen." Talk about the number problem that is written on the card. Ask students to find 14 objects in the classroom and bring them back to share with the group. Give each one a chance to tell about the objects he or she chose. Ask students to practice making number sentences with the objects they chose. To conclude, put 14 objects in the middle of your circle, talk about what groups make 14, and ask students to practice making the number 14 in the air.

Building Knowledge and Comprehension

Print a blank number sentence at the bottom of a sheet of paper "_____+_____=_____." Make and distribute a copy of the page for each student. Share Math Card 14 with students and ask them to make a number 14 in the air with their pointer fingers. Give students flag stickers or have them draw 14 flags on the paper. Tell them to think about two groups that will make 14. Direct their attention to the number sentence on the page. Tell students to fill in the number sentence to show how they grouped the flags. Ask students to point to the numbers while you read the number sentence to them. If using Math Cards 1–20, save each student's "fourteen" page in a folder so that he or she can make a book of the numbers 1–20. Keep the completed books in a class library for students to read.

Time to Differentiate!

For English language learners, scaffold the Language Development lesson by providing oral models for the discussion. Model how to tell about the objects you chose from the room. Then prompt students to follow your model. For example, say, "I have 14 yellow pencils. I picked them from the math center." Then guide students in using your model.

For below-level students, scaffold the Language Development lesson. Provide students with two groups of objects—one with the correct quantity and one with an incorrect quantity. Help students count each group of objects and identify which group matches the number for this lesson. Then discuss the objects as a group.

PHOTO CREDIT: © 2002 PHOTODISC

14
fourteen

$$\begin{array}{r} 10 \\ +\ 4 \\ \hline 14 \end{array}$$

fifteen

Activating Prior Knowledge

Show students Math Card 15. Ask them to look closely at the picture and describe what they see. Talk with students about what an acorn is and where a person could find one. Tell them that the number on the card is a number 15 and talk about the number. Tell them that there are 15 acorns in the picture. Have students count the acorns while you point to them. Tell students that you would like them to learn how to make a number 15. Model on the board or on a sheet of chart paper how to write a number 15. Ask students to practice making the number 15 in the air with their pointer fingers. Give students an opportunity to practice making the number 15 by providing a number-making center in the classroom. For example, have students practice making the number 15 out of fabric scraps.

Language Development

Ask students to sit in a circle near you. Direct students' attention to the number 15 at the top of the card. Ask them to make a number 15 in the air using their pointer fingers. Talk about how to spell *fifteen* and have students practice making the /f/ sound. Talk with students about the different ways to make 15. Using a manipulative like tile counters, model different ways to make 15. Use language like, "ten and five make fifteen," or, "six plus nine equals fifteen." Talk about the number problem that is written on the card. Discuss how the acorns are in two groups and create the same two groups using a math manipulative. Ask students to practice making number sentences with math manipulatives. To conclude, put 15 objects in the middle of your circle, talk about what groups make 15, and ask them to practice making the number 15 in the air.

Building Knowledge and Comprehension

Print a blank number sentence at the bottom of a sheet of paper "_____ + _____ = _____." Make and distribute a copy of the page for each student. Share Math Card 15 with students and ask them to make a number 15 in the air with their pointer fingers. Give students stickers or have them draw 15 objects on the paper. Tell them to make two groups that will make 15. Direct their attention to the number sentence on the page. Tell students to fill in the blanks with the appropriate numbers to make a number sentence. Ask students to point to the numbers while you read the number sentence to them. If using Math Cards 1–20, save each student's "fifteen" page in a folder so that he or she can make a book of the numbers 1–20. Keep the books in a class library for students to read.

Time to Differentiate!

For English language learners, provide extra assistance to help students complete the Building Knowledge and Comprehension activity. Draw a picture of each step on the board. Then talk students through each step as you point to the drawing on the board.

For below-level students, provide them with a model of the number 15 to refer to during these lessons. For example, write the number 15 on a sheet of paper and give one copy to each student. As you lead students through the lessons, encourage students to trace the number with their pointer fingers before making the number in the air.

15
fifteen

$$\begin{array}{r} 10 \\ + 5 \\ \hline 15 \end{array}$$

PHOTO CREDIT: © 2002 PHOTODISC

Activating Prior Knowledge

Show students Math Card 16. Ask them to describe what they see in the picture. Talk with students about what a watermelon is and during which season it is usually eaten. Ask students to tell about a time when they ate watermelon. Tell them that the number on the card is a number 16 and talk about the number. Have students count the watermelons while you point to them. Tell students that you would like them to learn how to make a number 16. Model how to write a number 16. Ask students to practice making the number 16 in the air with their pointer fingers. Give students opportunities to practice making the number 16 by providing a number-making center in the classroom. For example, have students practice making the number 16 using chalk on construction paper.

Language Development

Ask students to sit in a circle near you. Direct students' attention to the number 16 at the top of the card. Ask them to make a number 16 in the air using their pointer fingers. Talk about how to spell *sixteen* and have students practice making the /s/ sound. Talk about the different ways to make 16. Using color tiles, model different ways to make 16. Use language like, "ten and six make sixteen," or, "five plus eleven equals sixteen." Talk about the number problem that is written on the card. Ask students to find 16 objects in the classroom (e.g., beans, pennies, crayons) and bring them back to share with the group. Give each one a chance to tell about the objects he or she chose. To conclude, put 16 objects in the middle of your circle, talk about what groups make 16, and ask students to practice making the number 16 in the air.

Building Knowledge and Comprehension

Print a blank number sentence at the bottom of a sheet of paper "_____+_____=_____." Make and distribute a copy of the page for each student. Share Math Card 16 with students and ask them to make a number 16 in the air with their pointer fingers. Give each student a stamp and a stamp pad. Ask them to stamp groups on their paper that equal 16 when put together. For example, if a student was using a flower stamp and a star stamp, he or she could make nine flowers in one group and seven stars in the other group. Direct students' attention to the number sentence on the page. Tell them to fill in the blanks with the appropriate numbers to make a number sentence. Ask students to point to the numbers while you read the number sentence to them. If using Math Cards 1–20, save each student's "sixteen" page in a folder so that he or she can make a book of the numbers 1–20.

Time to Differentiate!

For English language learners, build their vocabulary for the Activating Prior Knowledge lesson. Point to and name the objects on the card. Provide some describing words. If possible, bring in some watermelon for students to feel and taste.

For below-level students, scaffold the Activating Prior Knowledge lesson by providing a model for students to follow as they practice making the number 16. For example, use a highlighter to write the number on chart paper and then ask students to trace the number in pencil.

PHOTO CREDIT: © 2002 PHOTODISC

16
sixteen

$$
\begin{array}{r}
10 \\
+\ 6 \\
\hline
16
\end{array}
$$

Activating Prior Knowledge

Show students Math Card 17. Ask them to look closely at the picture and describe what they see. Talk with students about what a beetle is. Tell them that the number on the card is a number 17 and talk about the number. Have students count the beetles while you point to them. Model on the board or on a sheet of chart paper how to write a number 17. Ask students to practice making the number 17 in the air with their pointer fingers. Give students an opportunity to practice making the number 17 by providing a number-making center in the classroom. For example, have students practice making the number 17 out of straws.

Language Development

Ask students to sit in a circle near you. Direct students' attention to the number 17 at the top of the card. Ask them to make a number 17 in the air using their pointer fingers. Talk about how to spell *seventeen* and have students practice making the /s/ sound. Talk with students about the different ways to make 17. Using a manipulative like color tiles, model different ways to make 17. Use language like, "ten and seven make seventeen," or, "five plus twelve equals seventeen." Talk about the number problem that is written on the card. Ask students to find 17 objects in the classroom and bring them back to share with the group. Give each one a chance to tell about the objects he or she chose. Ask students to practice making number sentences with the objects they chose. To conclude, put 17 objects in the middle of your circle, talk about what groups make 17, and ask students to practice making the number 17 in the air.

Building Knowledge and Comprehension

Print a blank number sentence at the bottom of a sheet of paper "_____+_____=_____." Make and distribute a copy of the page for each student. Share Math Card 17 with students and ask them to make a number 17 in the air with their pointer fingers. Ask students to draw two groups of beetles. Tell them to think about two groups that make 17. For example, there could be 14 beetles in the first group and three beetles in the second group. Direct students' attention to the number sentence on the page. Tell them to fill in the blanks with the appropriate numbers to make a number sentence. Ask students to point to the numbers while you read the number sentence to them. If using Math Cards 1–20, save each student's "seventeen" page in a folder so that he or she can make a book of the numbers 1–20.

Time to Differentiate!

For English language learners, label with card with English words before you begin the lesson. Then point to and read each word before asking students to repeat it. Continue to add relevant words as you discuss the card and activate prior knowledge.

For below-level students, review the number 17 and show students several examples of that quantity. Show students how to point to and count the objects on the card. Then invite each student to point to and count the objects with you.

PHOTO CREDIT: © 2002 PHOTODISC

17
seventeen

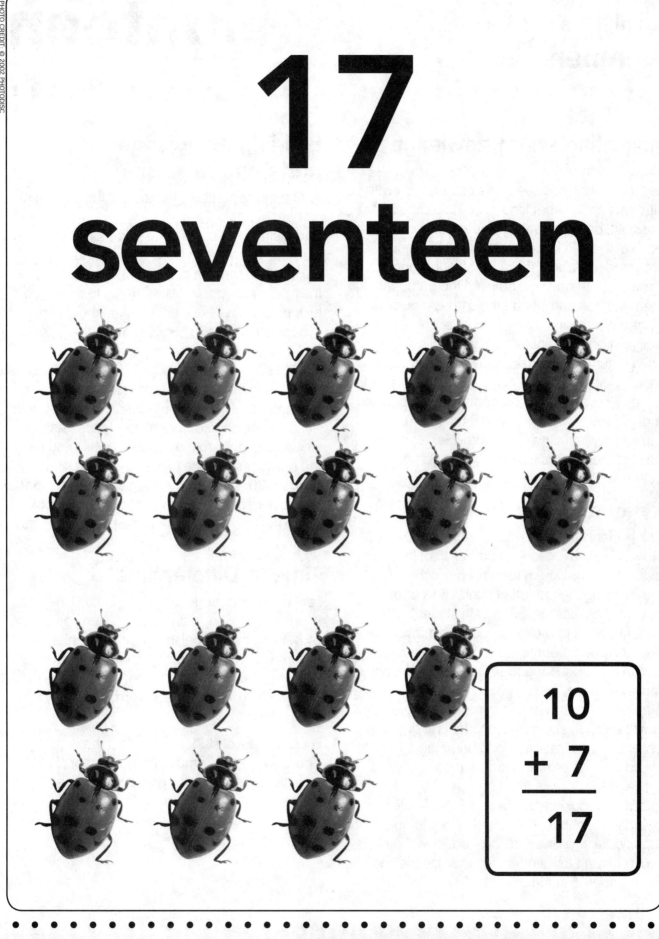

$$\begin{array}{r} 10 \\ + \ 7 \\ \hline 17 \end{array}$$

Unit 1 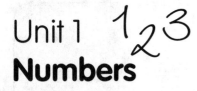 Numbers

eighteen

Activating Prior Knowledge

Show students Math Card 18. Ask them to describe what they see in the picture. Talk with students about what kind of ball is pictured. If possible, before showing students this card, ask each of them to bring a tennis ball to school. Talk with students about the sport of tennis and ask if any of them have ever played the game. Tell them that the number on the card is a number 18 and discuss it. Have students count the tennis balls while you point to them. Model how to write a number 18. Ask students to practice making the number 18 in the air with their pointer fingers. Give students an opportunity to practice making the number 18 by providing a number-making center in the classroom. For example, have students practice making the number 18 out of small cereal pieces.

Language Development

Ask students to sit in a circle near you. Direct students' attention to the number 18 at the top of the card. Ask them to make a number 18 in the air using their pointer fingers. Talk about how to spell *eighteen*. Talk with students about different ways to make 18. Using a manipulative like teddy bear counters, model different ways to make 18. Use language like, "ten and eight make eighteen," or "six plus twelve equals eighteen." Talk about the number problem that is written on the card. Ask students to find 18 objects in the classroom and bring them back to share with the group. If time is a concern, ask students to share in small groups. Ask students to practice making number sentences with the objects they chose. To conclude, put 18 objects in the middle of your circle, talk about what groups make 18, and ask students to practice making the number 18 in the air.

Building Knowledge and Comprehension

Print a blank number sentence at the bottom of a sheet of paper "_____+_____=_____." Make and distribute a copy of the page for each student. Share Math Card 18 with students and ask them to make a number 18 in the air with their pointer fingers. Ask students to draw two groups of balls. Tell them to think about two groups that make 18. For example, there could be 14 tennis balls in the first group and four footballs in the second group. Direct students' attention to the number sentence on the page. Tell them to fill in the blanks with the appropriate numbers to make a number sentence. Ask students to point to the numbers while you read the number sentence to them. If using Math Cards 1–20, save each student's "eighteen" page in a folder so that he or she can make a book of the numbers 1–20. Keep the books in a class library.

Time to Differentiate!

For English language learners, scaffold the Building Knowledge and Comprehension lesson by helping them label their number sentence pictures. Show students how we use the plural noun to show "more than one." Encourage students to use the correct word when they write their sentences.

For below-level students, scaffold the Building Knowledge and Comprehension lesson. Work with students in a small group to practice counting the objects correctly.

PHOTO CREDIT: © 2002 PHOTODISC

18
eighteen

$$\begin{array}{r} 10 \\ +\ 8 \\ \hline 18 \end{array}$$

Unit 1
Numbers

nineteen

Activating Prior Knowledge

Show students Math Card 19. Ask them to look at the picture and describe what they see. Talk with students about what a shell is. If possible, collect a variety of shells to share with students. Keep them at a class center for students to observe. Discuss where a person could find a shell. Share books about the ocean with your class. Discuss the number 19 with students. Have students count the shells while you point to them. Model how to write a number 19. Ask students to practice making the number 19 in the air with their pointer fingers. Give students an opportunity to practice making the number 19 by providing a number-making center in the classroom. For example, have students practice making the number 19 out of pipe cleaners.

Language Development

Ask students to sit in a circle near you. Direct students' attention to the number 19 at the top of the card. Ask them to make a number 19 in the air using their pointer fingers. Talk about how to spell *nineteen* and have students practice making the /n/ sound. Talk with students about the different ways to make 19. Using a manipulative like color tiles, model different ways to make 19. Use language like, "ten and nine make nineteen," or, "seven plus twelve equals nineteen." Talk about the number problem that is written on the card. Ask students to find 19 objects in the classroom and bring them back to share with the group. If time is a concern, ask students to share in small groups. To conclude, put 19 objects in the middle of your circle, talk about what groups make 19, and ask students to practice making the number 19 in the air.

Building Knowledge and Comprehension

Print a blank number sentence at the bottom of a sheet of paper "_____+_____=_____." Make and distribute a copy of the page for each student. Share Math Card 19 with students and ask them to make a number 19 in the air with their pointer fingers. Give students 19 shell shapes. Tell them to think about two groups that make 19. For example, there could be 14 shells in the first group, and five shells in the second group. Direct students' attention to the number sentence on the page. Tell them to fill in the blanks with the appropriate numbers to make a number sentence. Ask students to point to the numbers while you read the number sentence. If using Math Cards 1–20, save each student's "nineteen" page in a folder so that he or she can make a book of the numbers 1–20.

Time to Differentiate!

For English language learners, scaffold the Language Development lesson by providing oral models for the discussion. Model how to tell about the objects you chose from the room. Then prompt students to follow your model. For example, say, "I have 19 yellow pencils. I picked them from the math center." Then guide students in using your model.

For below-level students, scaffold the Language Development lesson. Provide students with two groups of objects—one with the correct quantity and one with an incorrect quantity. Help students count each group of objects and identify which group matches the number for this lesson. Then discuss the objects as a group.

PHOTO CREDIT: © 2002 PHOTODISC

19
nineteen

$$
\begin{array}{r}
10 \\
+\ 9 \\
\hline
19
\end{array}
$$

Unit 1
Numbers

twenty

Activating Prior Knowledge

Show students Math Card 20. Ask them to look at the picture and describe what they see. Talk with students about where a person would find ducks like the ones that are pictured. If possible, before showing students this card, bring in a small collection of different rubber ducks and keep them at a class center. Read books about ducks to your class. Discuss the number 20 with students. Have students count the ducks while you point to them. Model on the board or on a sheet of chart paper how to write a number 20. Ask students to practice making the number 20 in the air with their pointer fingers. Give students an opportunity to practice making the number 20 by providing a number-making center in the classroom. For example, have students practice making the number 20 with blocks.

Language Development

Ask students to sit in a circle near you. Direct their attention to the number 20 at the top of the card. Ask them to make a number 20 in the air using their pointer fingers. Talk about how to spell *twenty* and that it begins with a blend sound. Have students practice making the /tw/ sound. Talk about the different ways to make 20. Talk about how two groups of 10 make 20. Using a manipulative like color tiles, model different ways to make 20. Use language like, "ten and ten make twenty," or, "eight plus twelve equals twenty." Talk about the number problem that is written on the card. Ask students to work in pairs to show how they can make 20. For example, if they put all of their hands together, they will have 20 fingers. To conclude, put 20 objects in the middle of your circle, talk about what groups make 20, and ask students to practice making the number 20 in the air.

Building Knowledge and Comprehension

Print a blank number sentence at the bottom of a sheet of paper "_____ + _____ = _____." Make and distribute a copy of the page for each student. Share Math Card 20 with students and ask them to make a number 20 in the air with their pointer fingers. Provide students with a group of 20 stickers. Tell them to think about two groups that will make 20. For example, there could be 14 stars in the first group and six stars in the second group. Tell them to put the stickers in two groups on the paper to make 20. Direct their attention to the number sentence on the page. Tell students to fill in the blanks with the appropriate numbers to make a number sentence. Ask students to point to the numbers while you read the number sentence. If using Math Cards 1–20, save each student's "twenty" page in a folder so that he or she can make a book of the numbers 1–20. Keep the completed books in a class library for students to read.

Time to Differentiate!

For English language learners, provide extra assistance to help students complete the Building Knowledge and Comprehension activity. Draw a picture of each step on the board. Then talk students through each step as you point to the drawing on the board.

For below-level students, provide them with a model of the number 20 to refer to during these lessons. For example, write the number 20 on a sheet of paper and give one copy to each student. As you lead students through the lessons, encourage students to trace the number with their pointer fingers before making the number in the air.

20
twenty

$$\begin{array}{r} 10 \\ +10 \\ \hline 20 \end{array}$$

PHOTO CREDIT: © 2002 PHOTODISC

Unit 1 Numbers

Introductory Lesson—Part A

Objectives

Pre-K Standard 5.13: Students use visual and verbal cues, including pictures, to comprehend new words and stories.

K–2 Standard 5.1: Students use mental images based on pictures and print to aid in comprehension of text.

Skills

- observing different aspects of a text
- sharing observations orally
- understanding the connection between amounts and written numbers
- understanding number sentences

Materials

- Math Cards 1–20
- 10 sheets of chart paper
- markers

Word Study

- adding
- amount
- count
- notice
- number
- observation
- see

Comprehension and Skills

Part 1: Lesson Length: approx. 15 minutes

1. Show students Math Card 1.
2. Point out the number "1" at the top of the card. Remind students of the previous lessons in which they practiced writing numbers 1–20.
3. Point to the word *one*. Ask students to predict what that word might be. It might be worthwhile to point out that when reading the word *one* aloud, it does not sound the way a reader would expect.
4. Ask students to help you identify the picture on Math Card 1. Ask, "What do you notice about the picture?" They might notice that there is only one object (a toy train), and it is made of wood. They might also connect the picture to a toy they have at home. Remind students that making observations about something they see or read will help them understand it.
5. Continue with Math Card 2. Talk about the "2" and the word *two* at the top of the card. Ask students what they notice about the picture on the card.
6. Before showing Math Card 3, ask students to make a prediction. Ask, "How many objects do you think you will see on the next card?" Students should notice that there is a pattern. On the "three" card, there will be a picture of three objects.
7. Repeat this with Math Cards 4 and 5.

Introductory Lesson—Part A *(cont.)*

Comprehension and Skills

Part 2: Lesson Length: approx. 20 minutes

1. Show students Math Cards 6–10.

2. As you show each card, ask students to share their observations about the pictures on the cards. Ask questions that will prompt students to share their observations, such as:

   - Does this picture remind you of something in your life?

   - What are the important details in this picture?

   - Do you think the picture is missing anything?

   - What else could be pictured to represent the card's number?

Comprehension and Skills

Part 3: Lesson Length: approx. 20 minutes

1. Display five sheets of chart paper across the board. Explain to students that they are going to help you make a book that represents numbers. Today they will work on numbers 1–5.

2. On each sheet of chart paper, write a number. Write both the numeral and the number word, as is shown on Math Cards 1–5. Have students help after you have modeled the process.

3. Ask students to help you create a picture that represents the number on the card. Remind students of their previous observations about Math Cards 1–5, specifically that each card has pictured objects in the same amount as the number shown on the card.

4. It might be more efficient to draw only an outline of the object. Groups of students can color in the pictures during the center activity.

Comprehension and Skills

Part 4: Lesson Length: approx 20 minutes

1. Repeat the same process with numbers 6–10. On each sheet of chart paper, write both the numeral and the number word.

2. Ask students to help you create a picture that represents the number on the card.

Assessment

Choose one card from Math Cards 11–20. Ask students to share their observations about the pictures on the card.

Unit 1
Numbers

Focus Lesson

Objectives

Pre-K Standard 5.13: Students use visual and verbal cues, including pictures, to comprehend new words and stories.

K–2 Standard 5.1: Students use mental images based on pictures and print to aid in comprehension of text.

Skills

- visualizing information
- filling in missing information
- predicting information

Materials

- Math Cards 1–10
- chart paper
- marker

Word Study

- number
- see
- visualize

Comprehension and Skills

Part 1: Lesson Length: approx. 20 minutes

1. Show students Math Card 1. Review the word *one*. Point to the picture of the wooden train. In order for students to fill in "missing information" about a complete picture, you will need to ask questions to help them visualize additional information.

2. Following are examples of questions for Math Card 1:

   - Have you ever played with a similar kind of toy?
   - If this toy came with other toys, what else might the set include?
   - Would you like to have this toy? Why or why not?
   - Can you think of other toys that are similar to this one?

3. Review the word and number at the top of each card. Spend a few minutes discussing each card.

4. Each time you show each card, ask students questions that might elicit additional information about the picture. These questions should prompt them to think about the math card in a new and different way. Examples of questions for Math Card 2 include the following:

   - How does a pineapple feel when you touch it?
   - Have you ever eaten a pineapple?
   - What does it taste like?
   - What shape is a pineapple?

Focus Lesson *(cont.)*

Comprehension and Skills

Part 2: Lesson Length: approx. 15 minutes

1. Show students Math Card 3. Some examples of questions for Math Card 3 include the following:
   - What kind of dog do you see?
   - What might its bark sound like?
   - Do you think this dog can run fast?
   - Would you like this dog as a pet? Why or why not?

2. Show students Math Card 4. Some examples of questions for Math Card 4 include the following:
   - Have you ever eaten a strawberry?
   - How can you describe its taste?
   - How does a strawberry feel when you touch it?

3. Show students Math Card 5. Some examples of questions for Math Card 5 include the following:
   - How big do you think these stuffed teddy bears are?
   - What would its fur feel like?
   - Would you like these for toys? Why or why not?

Comprehension and Skills

Part 3: Lesson Length: approx. 20 minutes

1. Continue the same process with Math Cards 6–10.

2. Ask questions similar to those in Parts 1 and 2 of the lesson.

Comprehension and Skills

Part 4: Lesson Length: approx. 15 minutes

1. Display Math Cards 1–10 in order somewhere in the room. Ask, "What card will come next in this series?" Students should understand that "eleven" would be the next card.

2. Ask, "What kinds of objects might be pictured on Math Card 11?" Make a list of student predictions on chart paper.

Time to Differentiate!

For above-level students, have each one create a short story about one of the cards. Remind students to think about the questions you discussed as a class.

Assessment

The discussions of each math card serve as an ongoing assessment in this lesson. You should see students gradually strengthen their skills in visualizing and filling in missing information as they participate in class discussions.

Unit 1
Numbers

Center Activities

Objectives

Pre-K Standard 5.13: Students use visual and verbal cues, including pictures, to comprehend new words and stories.

K–2 Standard 5.1: Students use mental images based on pictures and print to aid in comprehension of text.

Center #1: Number Game

Materials

- sets of at least 15 index cards, with a 1, 2, or 3 written on each card
- cubes, tiles, or blocks for counting

Comprehension and Skills

1. Pair up students and give a set of index cards (with a 1, 2, or 3 on each card) to each partner group. The set should contain at least 15 index cards. Tell students to put the stack of cards face down between them. They should also have cubes, blocks, or tiles for counting.

2. The object of the game is to reach or pass the number 10. When each player has a turn, he or she takes a card from the top of the pile, looks at its number (1, 2, or 3), and then takes the same number of cubes, blocks, or tiles.

3. The other student will get a turn and repeat the same process.

4. During the second round, the player will take a second card. After the student takes a card from the stack, he or she will take the same number of cubes and add that card's number to the first card's number. The student should count the cubes aloud and tell his or her partner what the total is.

5. The game is over when one player reaches or exceeds 10. The game can be repeated several times.

6. Many variations can be added to this game to make it more challenging. Students could write number sentences as they are playing the game. These number sentences should represent the addition that happens throughout the game. Another variation is having students play until they reach or exceed 20. Finally, students may also play this game as a subtraction game. They could start the game with 10 cubes, and each card will indicate how many cubes to be take away to try to reach zero first.

Center Activities *(cont.)*

Center #2: Three Pictures

Materials

- large sheets of drawing paper
- crayons, markers, or colored pencils

Comprehension and Skills

1. Place large sheets of drawing paper and coloring materials in the center area. Show students how to fold the drawing paper into three equal sections.

2. Tell students that they are going to create three pictures of one topic. Give them a list of topics from which to choose. You may want to use topics that you are studying in class. Ideas for topics include the following:
   - making an ice cream sundae
   - leaving school at the end of the day
   - playing soccer
   - riding a scooter
   - having a birthday party
   - going to the movies

3. Explain to students that they are going to draw three pictures to represent the topic. They should draw them in the order in which they occur.

4. At another time, you may show these pictures to the rest of the class. Keep the third and final picture hidden, and ask students to predict what the student might have drawn in the last box.

Center #3: Number Books

Materials

- Math Cards 1–10
- blanks sheets of paper
- drawing materials
- student copies of Activities 1–10 (pages 78–87)

Comprehension and Skills

1. This activity may be done over the course of several days. At the center area, leave drawing paper and coloring materials for students. You might also want to leave Math Cards 1–10 so that students have an example to follow.

2. Students will create their own small books of numbered pages. Each student will need 10 sheets of drawing paper. On each sheet of paper, the student will write the number as a numeral and a word, and then draw a picture(s). Remind students that the pictured objects should match the number they are representing. Staple these pages together when they have finished all 10 sheets.

3. As students finish the project, they should work on Activities 1–10. These pages can be done independently or with another student at the center who is also finished with his or

Unit 1 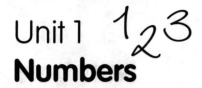 Numbers

Introductory Lesson—Part B

Objectives

Pre-K Standard 6.1: Students understand sequence of events.

K–2 Standard 6.3: Students know setting, main characters, main events, sequence, and problems in stories.

Skills

- understanding the importance of order in texts
- recognizing chronological, logical, or sequential order
- reviewing numbers 11–20
- writing numbers 11–20

Materials

- Math Cards 11–20
- chart paper
- marker
- chalkboard or whiteboard
- chalk or whiteboard markers
- peanut butter and jelly sandwich ingredients (peanut butter, bread, jelly, knife, plate) Note: Remember to consider students' food allergies.
- writing paper
- pencils
- 20 small objects for counting

Word Study

- chronological
- count
- number
- order
- sequential

Comprehension and Skills

Part 1: Lesson Length: approx. 15 minutes

1. Have students volunteer to discuss their typical morning routines. In what order do they complete their daily tasks such as brushing their teeth and eating breakfast?

2. Once students have shared, discuss what *chronological order* means. When recalling events that took place, chronological order is the order in which these events occurred.

3. Allow students to verbally recall their favorite vacations, arranging the details in chronological order.

Introductory Lesson—Part B (cont.)

Comprehension and Skills

Part 2: Lesson Length: approx. 15 minutes

1. Place the sandwich ingredients on a table for all the students to see.

2. Ask students, "What is the first thing you must do when you make a peanut butter and jelly sandwich?" Write the first step on a sheet of chart paper titled "How to Make a Peanut Butter and Jelly Sandwich."

3. Ask students to help you write each numbered step to describe the process.

4. Follow the steps to make the sandwich.

5. Ask, "Is it important to follow these steps in the correct order?" Let students think about this question until the next part of this lesson.

Comprehension and Skills

Part 3: Lesson Length: approx. 15 minutes

1. Write "How to Make a Peanut Butter and Jelly Sandwich" on chart paper.

2. Remind students of your earlier question about following these steps in the correct order.

3. Take the initial numbered list and cut out each step. Then show students how you can put those steps in various orders by taping them to a sheet of chart paper.

4. Ask, "Does changing the order of the list make a difference?" Compare the two lists. Show students that this list must be written and followed in order. It is a sequential text. Write the word *sequential* on a sheet of chart paper. Explain that *sequential* means that something describes one idea or step after another in a specific order.

Comprehension and Skills

Part 4: Lesson Length: approx. 15 minutes

1. Give each student a sheet of lined paper and a pencil.

2. Display Math Cards 11–20. Review each number, 11–20, and use a sheet of chart paper to model how to write each number correctly. After showing students how to write each number, show them the amount of the number by counting out small objects. For example, show students how to write the number 14 and then count out 14 objects. Ask students to help you count.

3. Give students a chance to practice writing these numbers independently.

Assessment

Ask students to help you write a chronological text about a recent special event in the classroom, such as a field trip, holiday celebration, or school festival. Then ask them to help you write a sequential text about a familiar routine in your classroom, such as the following:

- how to line up for recess
- how to return a book to the library
- how to ask for help

Unit 1
Numbers

Focus Lesson

Objectives

Pre-K Standard 6.1: Students understand sequence of events.

K–2 Standard 6.3: Students know setting, main characters, main events, sequence, and problems in stories.

Skills

- understanding the importance of order in texts
- recognizing chronological, logical, or sequential order
- reviewing numbers 11–20
- writing numbers 11–20
- recognizing number sentences
- connecting number sentences to functions
- developing an understanding of place value

Materials

- Math Cards 11–20
- chalkboard or whiteboard
- chalk or whiteboard markers
- chart paper
- marker

Word Study

- addition
- chronological
- equal
- logical
- number sentence
- order
- predict
- sequential

Comprehension and Skills

Part 1: Lesson Length: approx. 15 minutes

1. Show students Math Card 11.
2. Point out the number "11" at the top of the card. Remind students of the previous lessons in which they read cards about numbers 1–10.
3. Point to the word *eleven*. Ask students to use their knowledge of letters and letter sounds to predict what that word might be.
4. Ask students to identify the picture on Math Card 11. Ask, "How are the pictures displayed?" Students might notice that the picture shows a group of 10 objects with a single object underneath the group of 10. They might make the connection to the number sentence on the card (10 + 1 = 11). Explain that the author probably grouped 10 objects together so that the reader could see the connection between 10 and 11. This is an example of logical organization in a text.
5. Explain that Math Card 11 is an example of logical organization because the author placed the pictures in an order that would make the most sense to the reader. Talk about the definition of *logical*.

Focus Lesson (cont.)

Comprehension and Skills

Part 2: Lesson Length: approx. 20 minutes

1. Continue with Math Card 12. Talk about the number 12 and the word *twelve* at the top of the card. Have students help you read the word aloud.

2. Point out the pattern of the pictures. There are 10 objects grouped together, and the two remaining objects are placed to the side. Again, this logical organization reinforces the connection between 10 and 12.

3. Before showing Math Card 13, ask students to make a prediction. Ask, "What will the next card be?" Students should notice that there is a pattern and predict that the next card will show 13. Comment that the Math Cards are sequential because they come in numbered order.

4. Repeat the same process for Math Cards 14–15.

5. Then show students Math Cards 16–20, one at a time. As you show each card, ask students to help you read the number and word at the top of the card. Students should also point out any patterns they see in the pictures on each card.

Comprehension and Skills

Part 3: Lesson Length: approx. 20 minutes

1. Display Math Card 11. Comment that the card is be an example of sequential order (because it appears in numerical order with other cards) and logical order (because the pictures are logically placed together to show relationships to the number 10). Ask them to think of how they might make Math Card 11 an example of chronological order.

2. Have students help you create a chronological story about Math Card 11.

3. Use a sheet of chart paper and a marker to draft a chronological story about the 11 pails and shovels shown on Math Card 11. It might tell the story of 11 children waking up in the morning and deciding to visit the beach. It might also tell the story of 11 scientists who are combing the beach for a particular species.

4. After writing the story as a group, read it aloud to students. Ask them if there should be any additions or changes made to the text.

Time to Differentiate!

For above-level students, allow them to work independently to create their own chronological stories about Math Card 11. Or, you may wish to have them dramatize the stories in groups.

Assessment

Read a story aloud to students. Ask students to help determine if the story is in chronological, sequential, or logical order.

Unit 1 1 2 3
Numbers

Center Activities

Objectives

Pre-K Standard 6.1: Students understand sequence of events.

K–2 Standard 6.3: Students know setting, main characters, main events, sequence, and problems in stories.

Center #1: Sequential Books

Materials

- crayons, markers, or colored pencils
- colored construction paper
- drawing paper
- stapler
- Math Cards 11–20
- pencils

Comprehension and Skills

1. Tell students that they are going to make a sequential book by recreating Math Cards 11–20 and put them together to form a book.

2. Place drawing paper, coloring materials, and pencils at the center area.

3. Display Math Cards 11–20 so that students can be reminded of their format.

4. Model how to create a page to represent a number from 11 to 20. Remind students that each page should follow the same format as Math Cards 11–20; it should include a written word, a numeral, a number sentence, and pictures.

5. Students may need to work on this project over the course of several days.

6. When students are finished with all 10 pages, they can staple them together with two sheets of colored construction paper as front and back covers.

Center #2: Chronological Stories

Materials

- crayons, markers, or colored pencils
- drawing paper

Comprehension and Skills

1. Place drawing paper, coloring materials, and pencils at the center area.

2. Explain to students that they are going to create a chronological story.

3. Model how to fold a sheet of drawing paper into four squares.

4. Tell students that they are going to use pictures to tell the chronological story of a school day. Remind them that a chronological text describes events in the order in which they occurred.

5. Help students understand how to organize pictures to describe the day. For example, the first square will show an event at the beginning of the day, and the last square an event at the end of the day.

6. As a group, brainstorm ideas that can be included in the story of the day's events.

© Shell Education

Center Activities *(cont.)*

Center #3:
Activity Pages

Materials

- student copies of Activities 11–20 (pages 88–97)
- crayons, markers, or colored pencils

Comprehension and Skills

1. Students may work on Activities 11–20.
2. They may complete these activities independently or with partners.

Center #4:
Ordering Events

Materials

- drawing paper
- read-aloud book (optional)
- crayons, markers, or colored pencils

Comprehension and Skills

1. Place drawing paper and coloring materials in the center area.
2. Show students how to fold a sheet of paper into three equal parts.
3. Label each part "Beginning," "Middle," and "End."
4. Ask students to restate the facts and details of a recent story or event. You may choose to do a read-aloud and then ask students to illustrate information from the story. You can also choose a recent event and have them retell the highlights of that event. A field trip, class party, holiday celebration, or school assembly would work for this activity.
5. Emphasize the importance of describing the entire event or story by mentioning facts from the beginning, middle, and end. It is also equally important to organize the information in the correct order.

Unit 1
Numbers

Wrap-up

Introduction

The wrap-up activities tie together the skills that have been taught throughout the unit. They provide opportunities for students to show the skills they have learned within this unit.

Objectives

Pre-K Standard 5.13: Students use visual and verbal cues, including pictures, to comprehend new words and stories.

Pre-K Standard 6.1: Students understand sequence of events.

K–2 Standard 5.1: Students use mental images based on pictures and print to aid in comprehension of text.

K–2 Standard 6.3: Students know setting, main characters, main events, sequence, and problems in stories.

Materials

- Math Cards 1–20
- two read-aloud books (a chronological and sequential text)
- chalkboard or whiteboard
- chalk or whiteboard marker

Comprehension and Skills

Part 1: Lesson Length: approx. 15 minutes

1. Review Math Cards 1–20. Ask students to help you count aloud while you show each card.

2. Let students continue to count into the 20s, 30s, and so on until you are ready to have them stop.

3. Let students work with a partner to practice writing numbers from Math Cards 1–20.

Comprehension and Skills

Part 2: Lesson Length: approx. 15 minutes

1. Choose two short stories to share with students. One story should be organized chronologically and the other sequentially. Ask students to help you recognize which type of text you are reading.

2. Ask students to share their knowledge of chronological and sequential texts. Write their responses on the board.

3. Have students turn to a partner to share a fact and opinion about the stories you have read aloud.

Wrap-up *(cont.)*

Comprehension and Skills

Part 3: Lesson Length: approx. 15 minutes

1. Have students play the following game to test their observational skills and their visualizing strategies.

2. To play this game, ask students to sit on the rug. Have them close their eyes. Lightly tap one student on the shoulder. That student should open his or her eyes. Help that student stand up and very quietly walk outside the classroom. (He or she may also go into a large closet, bathroom, or adjoining room. Any location can be used as long as the rest of the students are unable to see him or her.)

3. As soon as the student is safely hidden, ask the rest of the students to open their eyes.

4. Students need to look around, make observations, and try to guess which student is missing.

5. To make the game more challenging, you can have two or more students leave the classroom while students' eyes are closed.

Comprehension and Skills

Part 4: Lesson Length: approx. 15 minutes

1. Another game involves changing something in the classroom environment. Make a change that you expect to be fairly noticeable to students. Some ideas include:
   - change the month on the calendar
   - move or remove a piece of furniture
   - hang something on the wall upside down
   - place something unusual somewhere in the classroom

2. You could make these changes during recess or before or after school and see what students observe when they walk in.

3. A final game might be to sort students by a "mystery" rule and see if the class is able to determine how you are sorting them. For example, ask the students who are wearing jeans to come to the front of the room. Ask, "What do these students have in common?" A variation of this game is to ask all students wearing jeans, excluding one student, to come to the front of the room. Ask, "Who else should be up here with these students?"

Draw **one** hat on each person.

Name _____

Draw **two** shoes on each person.

Unit 1 123
Numbers

Name _____

Draw a line from each set of **three** to the number **3**.

© Shell Education

Name _____

Color **four** in each group.

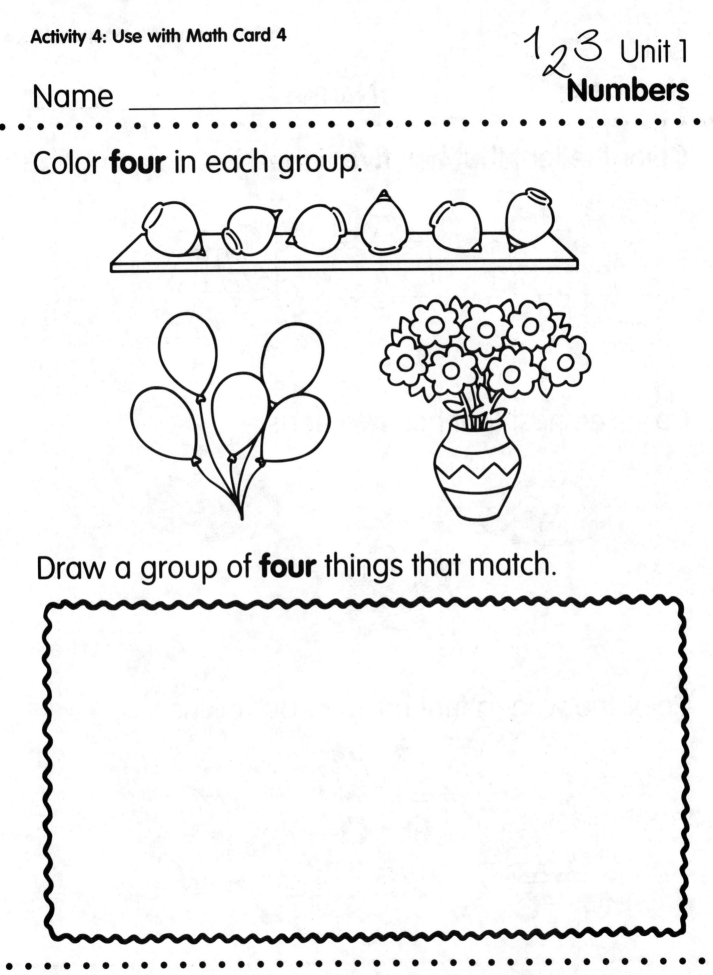

Draw a group of **four** things that match.

Color the tent that has **five** flags.

Color the nest that has **five** eggs.

Color the wagon that has **five** pumpkins.

Name _____

1 2 3 Unit 1
Numbers

Draw a line from each set of **six** to the number **6**.

Unit 1 123
Numbers

Name _____

Color the team that has **seven** players.

Name _____

Count the items in each group. If the group has **eight** items, write **8** in the box beside it.

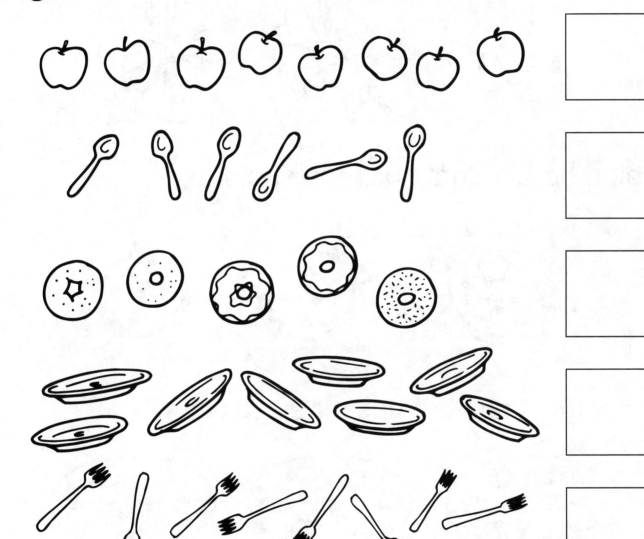

Unit 1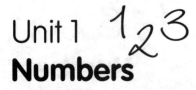
Numbers

Name _____

Color the flower that has **nine** petals.

Color the bug that has **nine** spots.

Color the plate that has **nine** cookies.

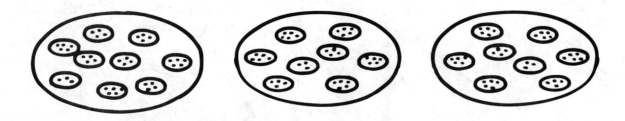

Draw **nine** beads on the string.

Name _____

Count and circle **ten** elephants.

Unit 1 1₂3
Numbers

Name _____

Count the items in each row.

Circle the row that shows **eleven**.

Unit 1
Numbers

Name _____

Count the jelly beans in the jar. How many jelly beans do you need to add to make **twelve**? Draw them.

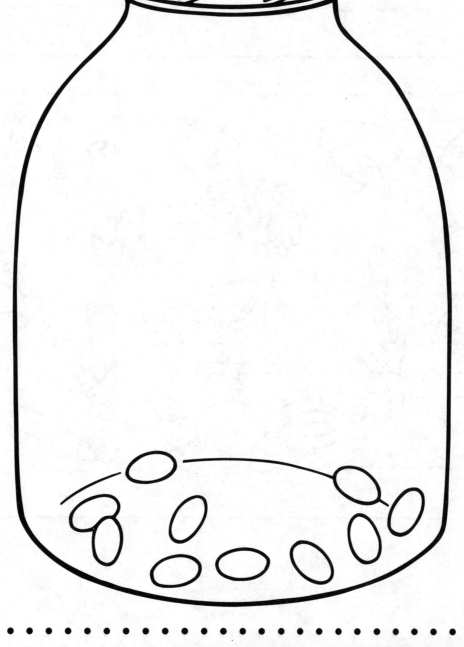

Unit 1 123
Numbers

Name _____

Draw a big circle around **thirteen** of the fish.

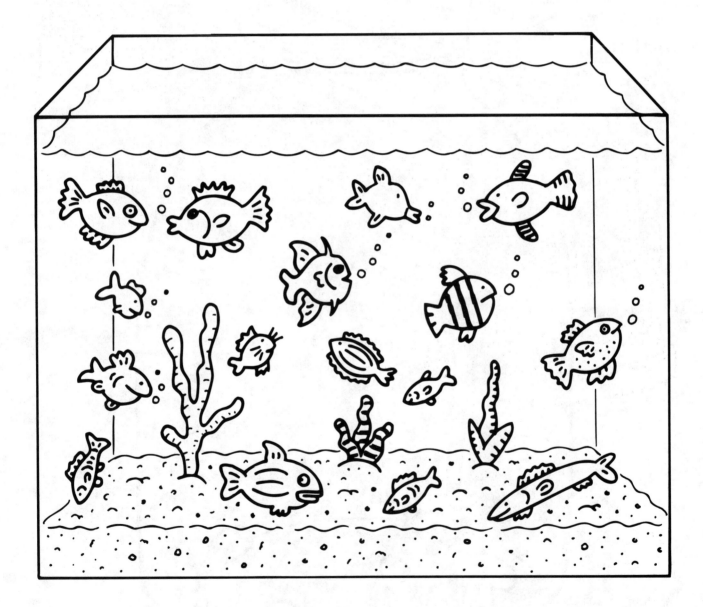

Name _____

Count the children in the bus. Draw enough children waiting at the stop to make **fourteen**.

Unit 1 1_23
Numbers

Name _____

Count the items in each row.

Circle the row that shows **fifteen**.

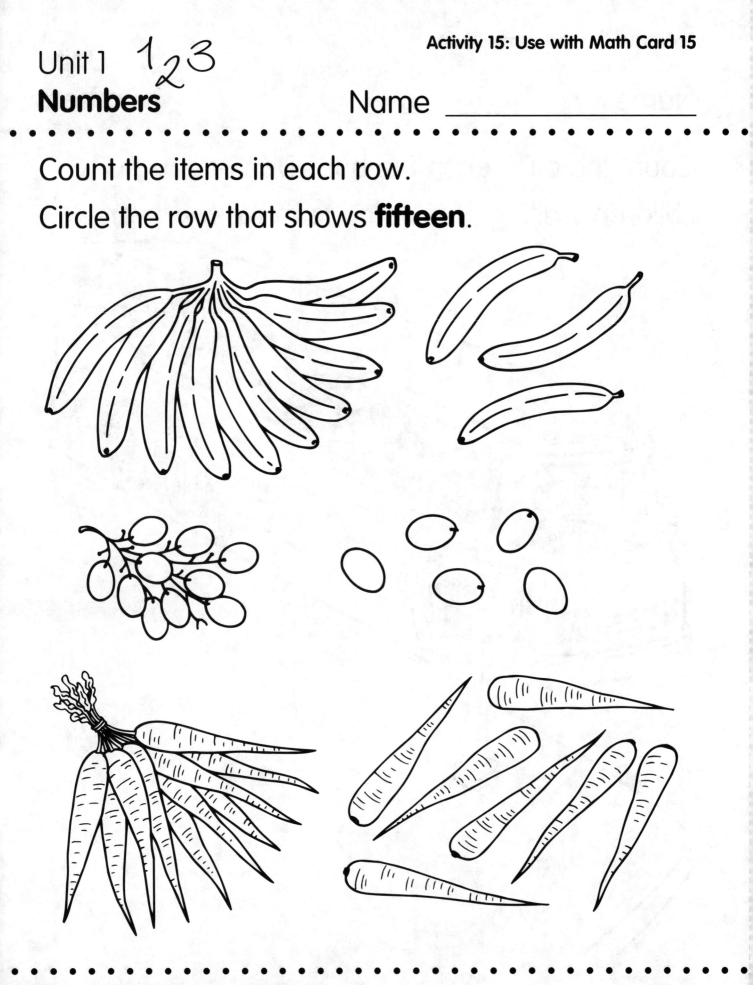

 #50453—*Start Exploring Nonfiction Reading in Mathematics*   © Shell Education

Name _____

123 Unit 1
Numbers

Count the slices of toast on the plate. How many slices of toast do you need to add to make **sixteen**? Draw them.

Unit 1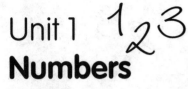
Numbers

Name _____

Color the set of ten stars on the left. Color enough stars on the right to make **seventeen**.

   © Shell Education

1₂3 Unit 1
Numbers

Name _____

Color **eighteen** butterflies.

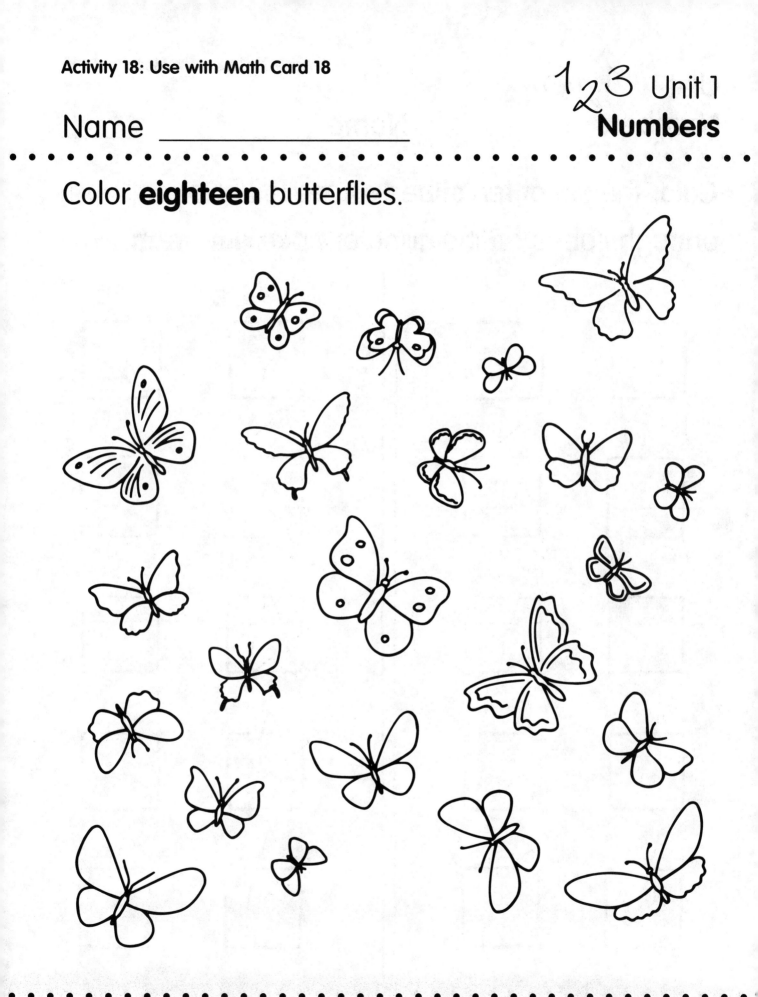

Unit 1
1 2 3
Numbers

Name _____

Color the set of ten cubes on the left. Color enough cubes on the right to make **nineteen**.

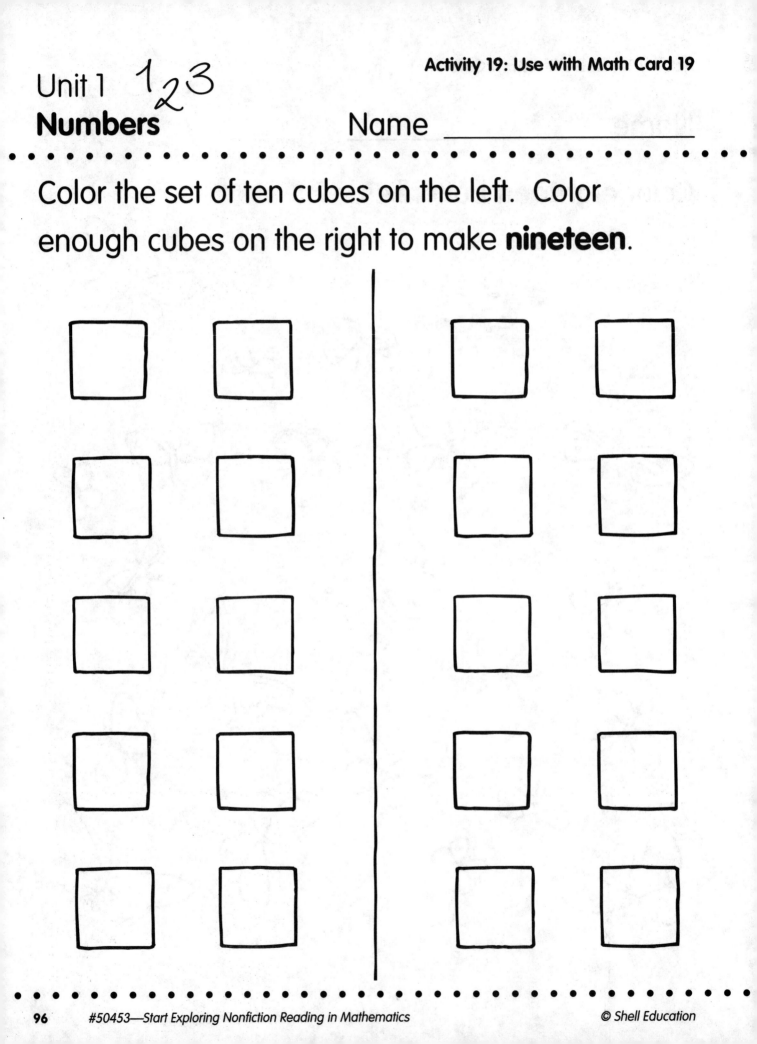

#50453—*Start Exploring Nonfiction Reading in Mathematics*   © *Shell Education*

Name _____

Help the pigs save their house from the wolf.

Add enough bricks to the wall to make **twenty**.

Numbers

Operations

Sort and Classify

Time and Money

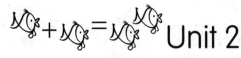
Introduction to Unit 2: Operations

This unit on operations is a great theme to introduce after the previous unit on numbers. Once students understand the basic concept of counting and are familiar with numbers 1–20, they can begin to understand how to set up and solve math problems. This unit focuses on understanding addition and subtraction. However, students will also learn to identify their purpose for reading different reading materials.

Skills Taught in This Unit

- brainstorming reasons that typeface is used
- recognizing typeface in texts
- locating typeface in texts
- understanding mathematical concepts
- understanding mathematical symbols
- distinguishing between various reading materials
- understanding that reading has a purpose
- understanding the connection between reading materials and a purpose for reading

Directions for the Teacher

You have many different options when teaching this unit. You can use the nonfiction text pages (Math Cards) and teach the content using the strategies that precede each card. Or, you can teach nonfiction skills and strategies by teaching the whole unit, starting with the introductory lesson, then teaching the focus lesson, and then following up with the center activities. This format repeats for the second lesson in the unit. Conclude the unit by teaching the wrap-up activity to tie all the nonfiction text and skills together.

Unit 2
Operations

$$\text{add} + \text{fish} = \text{fish}$$

add

Activating Prior Knowledge

Show students Math Card 21. Ask students to look at the picture and describe what they see. Talk about the two groups of oranges and the addition problem at the bottom of the card. Tell students that the word at the top of the card is *add*. Ask them if they know what it means to add numbers. Ask students to share with the class any numbers that they know how to add. Explain that adding is joining two groups together. When a person adds, he or she usually combines two or more groups of object to make one group. Talk about how the first group has three oranges and count the group of three oranges. Tell them there are four oranges in the second group and ask them to count this group of four oranges. Tell them that when the two groups are combined, they make a larger group of seven oranges. Count the seven oranges. Point out the way the addition problem is written at the bottom of the card.

Language Development

Share the card with students again. Ask them to read the word at the top of the card as you point to it. Tell students that rhyming words are words that sound the same. Ask students to think of words that rhyme with the word *add*. For example, *mad, sad, bad, fad*, and *pad*. Write the words that students come up with on the board or a sheet of chart paper. Discuss the ways to read a number problem. One way to read the problem at the bottom of the card is, "three plus four equals seven." Another way to read the problem is, "three and four make seven." Write both ways on the board or a sheet of chart paper. Read the number sentences several times while pointing to the words. Explain that when two numbers are added together, the answer is almost always bigger.

Building Knowledge and Comprehension

Ask students to sit in a circle on the floor. Share the card. Read the number problem at the bottom of the page. Tell them that you are going to pass a math manipulative around the circle—counting cubes work well. Ask them to take up to five cubes, but no more. After all students have cubes, ask the first two students to your right to put their cubes in the middle of the circle. Discuss the number of cubes in each group. For example, "Tommy has one cube and Alex has two cubes." Ask students if they know how to state the number problem. As a class, read the problem two ways. Push the cubes together to form one group and solve the problem. For example, if one student had one cube and another student had two cubes, the problem would read, "one and two make three," or, "one plus two equals three." After the problem has been solved, ask the next two students to place their cubes in the middle of the circle. Follow this same process until all students have had a chance to participate.

Time to Differentiate!

For English language learners, take time before beginning these lessons to review the English words for numbers. Practice counting in English as a group.

For below-level students, scaffold the Language Development lesson. Provide choices for the rhyming activity. For example, say to students, "Which word rhymes with *add—sad* or *pet*?"

PHOTO CREDIT: © 2002 PHOTODISC

add

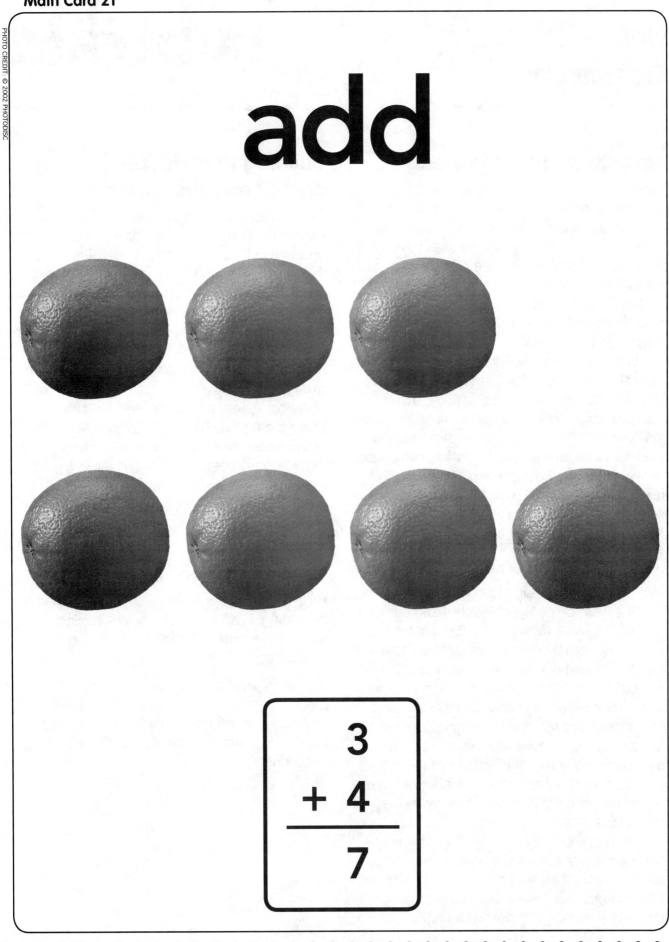

$$
\begin{array}{r}
3 \\
+\ 4 \\
\hline
7
\end{array}
$$

Unit 2
Operations

subtract

Activating Prior Knowledge

Share Math Card 22 with students. Ask them to describe what they see in the picture. Ask them to count the ice cream cones. Ask them if they have any idea why some of the cones have an "X" on them. Tell them that the word at the top of the card says *subtract*. Ask students if they know what *subtract* means. Remind students what it means to add things. Explain that to subtract means to take something away, or make the number less. Ask them to look at the picture and count the cones. Tell them that there are 12 ice cream cones. Five are being taken away; that is why they have an "X" on them. Cover the cones with an "X" on them with a sticky note to show that they are really being taken away. Ask students to count the number of cones left. Talk through the problem again. Tell them that you started out with 12 cones, five were taken away, and now there are seven cones left.

Language Development

Share the card with students again. Ask them to read the word at the top of the card, as you point to it. Ask students to look at the word at the top of the page. Tell them that the word begins with the letter "s" and ask them to practice making the /s/ sound. Have them practice writing the letter "s" in the air with their pointer fingers. Explain what it means to subtract something. Discuss the ways to read a number problem. One way to read the problem at the bottom of the card is, "twelve minus five equals seven." Another way to read the problem is, "twelve take away five leaves seven." Write both ways on the board or a sheet of chart paper. Read the number sentences several times while pointing to the words. Discuss how when subtracting a smaller number from a larger number, the answer is almost always less than the first number.

Building Knowledge and Comprehension

Ask students to sit in a circle on the floor. Share the card with students. Read the number problem at the bottom of the page. Tell students that you want them to help you make different number problems using counting cubes. Put six cubes in the middle of the circle and discuss the number of cubes with students. Ask the student to your right to take some cubes away from the middle. Discuss how many cubes are left. For example, "There were six cubes in the middle of the circle, Tommy took three cubes away. There are three cubes left." Verbally state the number sentence. For example, "six take away three leaves three," or "six minus three equals three." Put the six cubes back in the middle of the circle and give the next student a chance to participate. Follow these same steps until all students have a chance to participate.

Time to Differentiate!

For English language learners, take time before beginning these lessons to review the English words for numbers. Practice counting in English as a group.

For below-level students, preteach the /s/ sound. Model the sound for students. Remind them that it sounds like the hissing sound that a snake makes. Encourage students to practice making the sound.

PHOTO CREDIT: BRAND X PICTURES

subtract

$$\begin{array}{r} 12 \\ -\ 5 \\ \hline 7 \end{array}$$

Unit 2
Operations

Introductory Lesson—Part A

Objectives

Pre-K Standard 5.8: Students know that print appears in different forms and serves different purposes.

K–2 Standard 5.2: Students use meaning clues to aid comprehension.

Skills

- recognizing typeface in texts
- understanding mathematical concepts

Materials

- Math Cards 21–22
- 12 math cubes
- read-aloud book containing examples of typeface
- chart paper
- marker

Word Study

- add
- minus
- plus
- subtract
- typeface

Comprehension and Skills

Part 1: Lesson Length: approx. 20 minutes

1. Display Math Cards 21 and 22. Read the words *add* and *subtract* with students. Ask a volunteer to define the words.

2. Have students sit in a circle. Take 12 math cubes and place them on the rug. Ask students to help you count the cubes aloud. Point to each cube as you count aloud.

3. Divide the cubes into two groups of six. Ask students to help you count each group of cubes aloud. Remark that there is still the same number of cubes even though they have been divided into two groups.

4. Take two cubes from one group and two cubes from the other group of cubes. Ask students, "If I added two cubes and two cubes, how many will I have?" Place the cubes in the center of the circle and count them together aloud.

5. Tell students that adding objects (or numbers) together is an important part of math.

6. Place all 12 math cubes in the center of the circle again. Count them aloud so that students realize that there are still 12 cubes there.

7. Ask students, "If I take away four cubes from the 12 cubes, how many will I have left?" Place four cubes away from the group of 12 and together count them aloud.

8. Tell students that subtracting, or taking away, objects or numbers is another important part of math.

Introductory Lesson—Part A *(cont.)*

Comprehension and Skills

Part 2: Lesson Length: approx. 15 minutes

1. Find a book that contains one or more examples of typeface. If possible, choose a big book to read so that students can clearly see the typeface on the page. Explain that sometimes an author will make certain printed words or phrases look different from other words so that they stand out.

2. Begin reading the book aloud. Point to each word as you are reading.

3. As you are reading and you come across an example of typeface, stop to point it out. Tell them what this particular kind of typeface is called (e.g., italics, boldface). Share why the author may have included the typeface in this specific place in the text.

4. Continue reading aloud and sharing examples of typeface with students.

5. Make a list of different kinds of typeface on a sheet of chart paper. Include the name of each typeface and an example. You might want to include examples that were not in the book so that students can look for them while browsing through books.

Assessment

Choose another read-aloud book so that students can practice identifying typeface. If possible, choose a counting book to reinforce students' knowledge of numbers.

Unit 2
Operations

Focus Lesson

Objectives

Pre-K Standard 5.8: Students know that print appears in different forms and serves different purposes.

K–2 Standard 5.2: Students use meaning clues to aid comprehension.

Skills

- locating typeface in texts
- brainstorming reasons that typeface is used
- understanding mathematical symbols

Materials

- Math Cards 21–22
- chalkboard or whiteboard
- chalk or whiteboard markers
- chart paper
- marker
- lined paper
- pencils
- various books with examples of typeface (see Assessment)

Word Study

- add
- boldfaced print
- main idea
- minus
- number sentence
- plus
- sign
- subtract
- typeface

Comprehension and Skills

Part 1: Lesson Length: approx. 15 minutes

1. Display Math Card 21.
2. Point out the word at the top of the card. Ask students if they can identify the word. Sound it out and read it together as a group. Point out both the short /a/ and /d/ sounds to students.
3. Explain that the word *add* is written in boldfaced print.
4. Ask students, "Why do you think the author chose to write this word in boldfaced print?" If students do not have a reasonable answer, share your opinions about the author's intentions. (Perhaps the author wanted to make the word *add* stand out because it is the title. He or she could have also wanted the word *add* to stand out because it represents the main idea of the card.) Explain what is meant by a main idea.
5. Show students Math Card 22. Point out the word at the top of the card. Ask students if they can identify the word. Sound it out and read it together as a group.
6. Reiterate that *subtract* is written in boldfaced print. The author chose to have the word *subtract* stand out by changing its typeface. Review the potential reasons why the author might have made this choice.

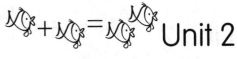
Focus Lesson *(cont.)*

Comprehension and Skills

Part 2: Lesson Length: approx. 15 minutes

1. Show students Math Cards 21 and 22. Talk about the number sentences at the bottom of these cards. Talk about the "+" and "-" symbols and how they correspond to the concepts of addition and subtraction.

2. Show students how number sentences are often written horizontally and vertically. Tell them that both mean the same thing. Write both types on the board so that they can see what both look like.

Comprehension and Skills

Part 3: Lesson Length: approx. 20 minutes

1. Distribute lined paper and pencils.

2. Use a sheet of chart paper to recreate Math Card 21. Ask students to help you decide on an object to draw, similar to the way the oranges are pictured on the card.

3. Draw two rows of the object. Count each row aloud with students. Review how to add two numbers together.

4. Ask students, "What number sentence can be written to represent this picture?" Model an appropriate response at first, if necessary. Have students write a horizontal and a vertical number sentence on their lined paper. Write a number sentence on the chart paper underneath the picture.

5. Repeat this process several times. Keep these sheets of chart paper in a place where students can look through them.

Comprehension and Skills

Part 4: Lesson Length: approx. 20 minutes

1. Distribute lined paper and pencils.

2. Use a sheet of chart paper to recreate Math Card 22. Ask students to help you decide on an object to draw, similar to the way the ice cream cones are pictured on the card.

3. Draw two rows of the object. Count each row aloud with students. Review how to subtract two numbers.

4. Ask students, "What number sentence can be written to represent this picture?" Model an appropriate response at first, if necessary. Have students write a horizontal and a vertical number sentence on their lined paper. Write a number sentence on the chart paper underneath the picture.

5. Repeat this process several times. Keep these pieces of chart paper in a place where students can look through them.

Time to Differentiate!

For above-level students, challenge them to write a simple story to represent the number sentence on one of the charts.

Assessment

Place students in pairs. Provide them with books that have examples of typeface. Ask them to find examples of typeface in the book. Bring the pairs back as a group, and ask each pair to share their typeface examples.

Unit 2
Operations

Center Activities

Objectives

Pre-K Standard 5.8: Students know that print appears in different forms and serves different purposes.

K–2 Standard 5.2: Students use meaning clues to aid comprehension.

Center #1: Recognizing Typeface

Materials

- various books containing examples of typeface
- sticky notes
- drawing paper

Comprehension and Skills

1. Leave various books containing examples of typeface in the center area. Leave sticky notes and drawing paper, as well. Tell students that they may look through books independently or with a partner. If they locate an example of typeface, they should place a sticky note on the page to mark it.

2. Tell students that they may use an example of typeface from one or more books to help them draw the typeface on a sheet of drawing paper. Emphasize that their drawings are only meant to be drafts. The purpose of the activity is for students to be able to practice recognizing typeface.

Center #2: Cube Pictures

Materials

- drawing paper
- groups of 12 math cubes
- crayons, markers, or colored pencils
- chart paper from Focus Lesson, Part 3

Comprehension and Skills

1. Place drawing paper, groups of 12 math cubes, coloring materials, and the chart paper from the Focus Lesson (Part 3) in the center area.

2. Explain to students that they are going to create pictures that resemble Math Cards 21 and 22.

3. Remind them of the pictures that were created as a group in the Focus Lesson. Explain that each page should have two rows of pictures of the same objects and a number sentence.

4. Students will be creating both an addition and a subtraction page. They should include "Add" or "Subtract" as a title on each page. Remind them of the connection between the picture and the number sentence. The number sentence should show that students are adding the two rows together, or subtracting objects by placing an "X" over each picture.

5. Students may use the math cubes to help them if necessary.

Center Activities *(cont.)*

Center #3:
Activity Pages

Materials

- student copies of Activities 21–22 (pages 118–119)

Comprehension and Skills

1. Read the directions to the activity pages.
2. Students may work on Activities 21–22. They may complete these activities independently or with partners.

Unit 2
Operations

Introductory Lesson—Part B

Objectives

Pre-K Standard 5.8: Students know that print appears in different forms and serves different purposes.

K–2 Standard 6.2: Students know the basic characteristics of familiar genres.

Skills

- distinguishing between various reading materials
- understanding that reading has a purpose
- understanding the connection between reading materials and a purpose for reading

Materials

- various reading materials (e.g., book, newspaper, magazine, menu, recipe, schedule, directions)
- chart paper
- marker

Word Study

- purpose
- reading material

Comprehension and Skills

Lesson Length: approx. 20 minutes

1. Display the various reading materials, and say, "People read books, but they also read many different kinds of materials. What kinds of materials do you or your family read?"

2. As students offer their responses, write them on a sheet of chart paper. (Sample answers: newspapers, magazines, comic books, maps, recipe books, letters, and mail)

3. Draw a small picture next to each written item on the chart paper. This way, students can associate the name with a visual image.

4. If students mention one of the materials that you brought in to class for this activity, share it with the class.

5. When students stop volunteering ideas, share all the materials you brought to class. Discuss what each item is for. Have students volunteer to sound out any words that they can identify on the reading materials.

6. Tell students that people read different materials for different reasons. Ask, "Would you read a newspaper to learn how to make cookies? Would you read a menu to learn about the current news?" Lead them to understand that each reading material satisfies a different purpose for reading.

Introductory Lesson—Part B *(cont.)*

Assessment

Ask students to sit in small groups and share the list of materials that are read in their homes. Tell them that they can also mention why they might read a particular material at home.

Unit 2
Operations

Focus Lesson

Objectives

Pre-K Standard 5.8: Students know that print appears in different forms and serves different purposes.

K–2 Standard 6.2: Students know the basic characteristics of familiar genres.

Skills

- understanding purposes for reading
- distinguishing between various reading materials

Materials

- Math Cards 21–22
- various reading materials (e.g., book, newspaper, magazine, menu, recipe, schedule, directions)
- list of reading materials created in Introductory Lesson B (page 110)
- math textbook
- survey

Word Study

- purpose
- reading materials

Comprehension and Skills

Part 1: Lesson Length: approx. 15 minutes

1. Review the list of reading materials that was created in Introductory Lesson B. Review the fact that different purposes for reading are satisfied by different reading materials.

2. Show students Math Cards 21 and 22. Ask, "Why might a reader be interested in these two cards?" Discuss this question as a group. Students might remark that a reader would want to know more about math, counting, addition, or subtraction. Tell them that most readers would be interested in these texts so that they could learn about something new (addition and subtraction).

3. Ask students, "Where would you expect to see text like Math Card 21 or 22?" Lead them to understand that this kind of information is likely to be found in a math textbook.

4. Show students a math textbook. Explain that a math textbook is a collection of math problems and examples. Math Cards 21 and 22 might be a part of a math textbook section on adding and subtracting.

5. Discuss the fact that textbook readers are interested in learning something new.

Focus Lesson (cont.)

Comprehension and Skills

Part 2: Lesson Length: approx. 15 minutes

1. Place the various reading materials on display in the classroom. Ask students a few questions to get them thinking about the different purposes for reading. Examples of questions follow:

   - Which material might you read if you wanted to know about today's weather?
   - Which material would you read just for fun?
   - Which material might help you understand how to build a toy?
   - Which material might you read if you wanted to learn something new?
   - Which material might help you find a friend's phone number?
   - Which material would you read if you enjoyed a particular author?
   - Which material might change your mind about something?
   - Which material might share the opinions of others?

2. Have students answer the following survey questions:

   - What do you read for fun at home?
   - What do you read at home that teaches you something new?
   - Is there a kind of reading material that you read every day?
   - What is your favorite kind of reading material?

Time to Differentiate!

For above-level students, have them use the data from the lesson to create a presentation. They may wish to create a graph, poster, or chart of the information.

Assessment

Let students share any interesting information they learned about themselves when completing the survey.

Unit 2
Operations

Center Activities

Objectives

Pre-K Standard 5.8: Students know that print appears in different forms and serves different purposes.

K–2 Standard 6.2: Students know the basic characteristics of familiar genres.

Center #1: Survey Fun

Materials

- classroom survey
- pencil

Comprehension and Skills

1. To prepare for this center, write or type each question of the student survey and leave room for answers. Include the following questions:

   - What do you read in this classroom for fun?

   - What book can you learn something from?

   - Where would you read directions to learn how to do something?

   - What book's pictures are interesting to you?

   - What book would you read because you like the author?

   It might be helpful to underline a word in each question so that students can focus in on the meaning of the question.

2. Explain to the class that in the learning center, they are going fill out a survey about classroom reading materials. Read each question aloud to students.

3. Depending on the skills of students, they may fill out the survey independently or with a partner.

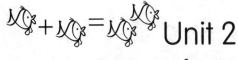
Center Activities (cont.)

Center #2:
Reading Material

Materials

- pencil
- index cards labeled *newspaper, menu, bus schedule, cereal box, book, comic book*
- examples of a newspaper, menu, bus schedule, cereal box, book, comic book
- drawing paper
- crayons, markers, or colored pencils

Comprehension and Skills

1. Leave the index cards, reading materials, drawing paper, and coloring materials at the center area.

2. Explain to students that they are going to get to create reading material from scratch.

3. Read each index card aloud. Review these reading materials by showing the examples that you have gathered. Students may use these examples while they are working. If students would like to create another kind of material that is not listed on a card, encourage them to do so.

4. These finished products can be displayed on a bulletin board in the classroom.

Unit 2
Operations

Wrap-up

Introduction

The wrap-up activities tie together the skills that have been taught throughout the unit. They provide opportunities for students to show the skills they have learned within this unit.

Objectives

Pre-K Standard 5.8: Students know that print appears in different forms and serves different purposes.

K–2 Standard 5.2: Students use meaning clues to aid comprehension.

K–2 Standard 6.2: Students know the basic characteristics of familiar genres.

Materials

- Math Cards 21–22
- any other Math Card that has boldface type
- lined paper
- pencils

Comprehension and Skills

Part 1: Lesson Length: approx. 15 minutes

1. Review Math Cards 21 and 22. Remind students of typeface and how the words *add* and *subtract* are in boldface type.

2. Find another *Start Exploring Nonfiction Reading* Math Card to share with students. Make sure that it has an example of typeface on it. (Most of the cards show an example of typeface because they have boldfaced words.)

3. Discuss the card with students. Ask them the following questions:

   - What kind of typeface do you recognize on this card?
   - Where is the typeface located on the card?
   - Why do you think the author decided to use a typeface for this text?
   - How does this typeface help the reader?
   - What would be your purpose for reading this card?
   - What kind of reading material might have text like this?

Wrap-up *(cont.)*

Comprehension and Skills

Part 2: Lesson Length: approx. 15 minutes

1. If you have a regularly scheduled independent or partner reading time, this activity may be used during that time. If students do not typically have time to read books on their own, this activity should be scheduled over the course of several days.

2. During each independent or partner reading time, ask students to choose a book that satisfies a specific purpose. Some suggestions include:

   - Find a book to read for fun.
   - Find a book to read to learn something new.
   - Find a book by an author that you enjoy.
   - Find a book that will teach you about _____.
   - Find a book that will tell you something new about a topic you already know about.
   - Find a book about a topic that is unfamiliar to you and your partner.

Unit 2
Operations

Name _____

Write a number sentence for each set of pictures.

Add the numbers.

+ _____

_____

_____

+ _____

_____

_____

Name _____

Write a number sentence for each set of pictures.
Subtract the numbers.

_____
− _____
_____

_____

_____
− _____
_____

_____

Numbers

Operations

Sort and Classify

Time and Money

Sort and Classify

Introduction to Unit 3: Sort and Classify

This unit teaches students how to organize information in efficient ways. Students will learn important vocabulary terms such as *shapes, triangle, circle, square, pattern, order*, and *graph*. In this unit, students will learn to connect prior knowledge to new information in texts, as well as relate new information to their own lives and experiences.

Skills Taught in This Unit

- organizing information
- recognizing a pattern
- recognizing a graph
- recognizing shapes
- making a pattern
- sorting objects
- creating a pattern
- creating a graph
- reading and locating information on a graph
- connecting prior knowledge to text
- creating visual images
- distinguishing different-size objects

Directions for the Teacher

You have many different options when teaching this unit. You can use the nonfiction text pages (Math Cards) and teach the content using the strategies that precede each card. Or, you can teach nonfiction skills and strategies by teaching the whole unit, starting with the introductory lesson, then teaching the focus lesson, and then following up with the center activities. This format repeats for the second lesson in the unit. Conclude the unit by teaching the wrap-up activity to tie all the nonfiction text and skills together.

Unit 3
Sort and Classify

shapes

Activating Prior Knowledge

Share Math Card 23 with students. Ask them to describe what they see. Ask students to look at the square. Say the word *square* and ask them to repeat after you. Point out the four sides of the square and how they are all straight. Have students count the sides with you. Ask students to look at the triangle. Say the word *triangle* and ask them to repeat after you. Point out the three sides of the triangle and how they also are all straight. Ask them if they see any other triangles in the picture. Now, direct students' attention to the circle. Say the word *circle* and ask them to repeat after you. Ask them to look at the shape of the circle. Ask them to think about what is different about the circle compared to the square and the triangle. Explain to students that the objects in the picture are shapes.

Language Development

Ask students to look at the card again. Tell them that the word at the top of the card is *shapes*. Ask them to read it with you while you point to it. Ask them what the word *shapes* starts with. Tell them that although the word begins with the letter "s," the first two letters make the beginning sound. Explain that when two letters make a new sound together, it is called a digraph. Make the /sh/ sound and ask them to repeat after you. Point out that /sh/ is the sound we make when we want someone to be quiet. Ask students to think of other words that begin with the /sh/ sound. Write the words on the board or a sheet of chart paper. Ask students to look at the words under the shapes. Tell them that the words are the names of the shapes above them. Point to the word *square* and read it to students. Ask them to read it with you. Discuss the sounds heard in the word. Follow these same steps with *triangle* and *circle*.

Building Knowledge and Comprehension

Share the card with students again. Ask them to read the word at the top of the card, and also read the words under the shapes while you point to them. Direct students' attention to the square. Ask them to draw a square with their pointer fingers. Tell them to look around the room and find other squares. Write the names of the objects students see on the board or a sheet of chart paper. Do the same thing with the triangle and the circle. Then take the class for a walk around the school. Look for shapes as you go. When a student finds a shape that you are looking for, allow each student to trace it with his or her finger, or ask students to draw it in the air with their pointer fingers. Look for all three shapes—circle, square, and triangle—around the school. This would also be a good time to introduce other shapes such as the oval and rectangle. Discuss the similarities and differences among all the shapes.

Time to Differentiate!

For English language learners, take time before beginning these lessons to review the English words for the different shapes presented in the lesson. Draw the shapes on the board or on chart paper and label them. Then say each word before asking students to repeat it.

For below-level students, scaffold the Building Knowledge and Comprehension lesson. Assign each student one shape to search for as you walk around the school. For additional support, you may wish to give each student a construction paper cutout of his or her assigned shape.

PHOTO CREDIT: SQUARE: DON STEVENSON/INDEXSTOCK IMAGERY/PICTUREQUEST; TRIANGLE: © DORLING KINDERSLEY; CIRCLE: CORBIS IMAGES/PICTUREQUEST

shapes

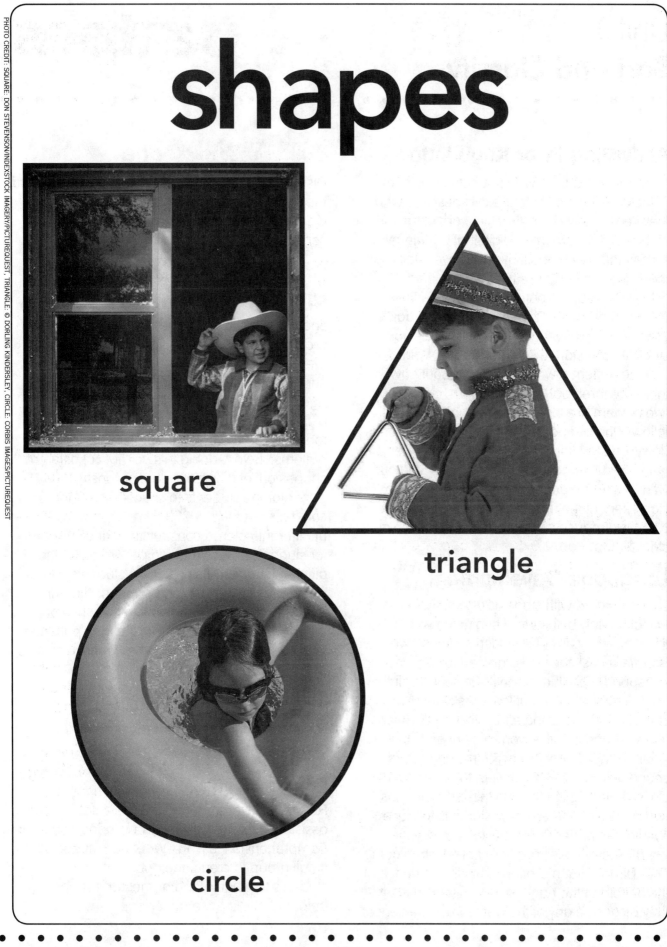

square

triangle

circle

Unit 3
Sort and Classify

pattern

Activating Prior Knowledge

Share Math Card 24 with students. Ask them to look closely at the picture and describe what they see. Tell students that the word at the top of the card is *pattern*. Explain that a pattern is something that repeats over and over. Tell them that a pattern can have two or more parts. Ask them to look at the pattern of flowers in the picture. Point to the zinnia and then the daisies. Point to each flower as you say its name so students can start to see the pattern. Point out that the pattern never ends. Talk about how there are three parts to the pattern, even though two of them are the same. The pattern is as follows: the first part is zinnia, the second part is daisy, and the third part is daisy. Ask students to help you make patterns with actions. Start out with a two-part pattern. For example, stomp, clap. Repeat the pattern several times. You may wish to introduce a three-part pattern, such as stomp, clap, clap.

Language Development

Share the card with students again. Ask them to look closely at the word beginning with "p" at the top of the card. Tell students that the word is *pattern*. Ask them to practice making the /p/ sound. Tell students to listen very carefully as you say the word out loud. Ask them what sound they hear at the end of the word. After they respond that the word *pattern* ends in the letter "n," ask them to practice making the /n/ sound. Read the word *pattern* together as a class. Point out to the class that the word has two syllables, *pat-tern*. Ask students to place two fingers under their chins as they say the word. The syllables are easy to feel when doing this. Direct students' attention to the sentence at the bottom of the page. Ask students to see if they recognize any of the words in the sentence.

Discuss the words that students recognize. Read the sentence to students while pointing to the words with a pointer. Ask students to read the sentence with you several more times.

Building Knowledge and Comprehension

Share the card with students again. Ask them to read the word *pattern* while you point to it. Ask them to read the sentence at the bottom of the card while you point to it. Discuss with students again what a pattern is. Read the pattern of flowers one more time. Tell students that together you are going to make a class book of patterns. Before doing this activity, cut different shapes out of different colors of construction paper for the students to choose from. You could also use 1/2" x 2" (1.5 cm x 5 cm) strips of different-colored construction paper. Model for students how to make a pattern out of the different shapes or strips. Give students a large sheet of white construction paper and ask them to make a pattern and glue it to the white paper. When students are done making their patterns, bind the pattern pages together to make a class book.

Time to Differentiate!

For English language learners, preview the names of the flowers pictured on the card. If possible, bring in some real flowers for students to look at and smell.

For below-level students, provide extra assistance for the Building Knowledge and Comprehension lesson. Work with students in a small group to create their patterns. Encourage students to point to and name each shape before identifying the pattern.

PHOTO CREDIT: © 2002 PHOTODISC

pattern

Do you see the **pattern**?

Unit 3
Sort and Classify

order

Activating Prior Knowledge

Share Math Card 25 with students. Ask them to look closely at the picture and describe what they see. Ask students if they know what the items in the picture are. If possible, bring in an example of the wooden dolls to share with your class. Explain to students that you are going to be discussing size and order. Choose three items in the classroom. Try to pick items with obvious variations in size. Ask students to help put the items in order from smallest to biggest. Then use the words from the card—*big, bigger,* and *biggest*—while naming the items in order. You could also mention the ordinal numbers that would be appropriate: first, second, and third. Next, ask three students to choose three more objects. This time name the order of the objects by saying small, smaller, and smallest. Add a few more objects and practice the ordinal numbers up to *tenth.*

Language Development

Show the card to students again. Ask students what the word at the top of the card begins with. Tell them that the word *order* begins with the letter "o" and ask them to practice making the long /o/ sound. This sound is r-controlled. Have students practice making the /or/ sound also. While pointing to the word *order,* read it out loud to students. Segment the word *order* (or-der) and ask students to repeat the word. Ask students to look at the words under the pictures. Tell students that the first word is *big.* Ask them if they notice anything similar between the first and second words, *big* and *bigger.* Ask them if they see any similarities between the first, second, and third words. Discuss with students how all three words have the base word *big,* and only the ending changes. Point to the words and have students read them with you.

Building Knowledge and Comprehension

Share the card with students. Read the word order at the top of the card and the words *big, bigger,* and *biggest* with students. Ask students to crouch down low to the ground. Ask them to repeat the word *big* after you say it. Tell students to get a little taller, and ask them to repeat the word *bigger* after you say it. Finally, ask students to reach up towards the sky as high as their hands can reach. Ask them to repeat the word *biggest* after you say it. Follow the same process, but start standing tall and say the word *small.* Ask students to get smaller, and finally ask them to get as low to the ground as they can and say the word *smallest.* Cut out of construction paper several shapes in different colors and sizes. Give each student six shapes and ask him or her to glue them to a larger sheet of construction paper in smallest to biggest order. Discuss the pictures as a class when finished.

Time to Differentiate!

For English language learners, preteach the comparitive words *big, bigger,* and *biggest.* Use students in the classroom to show the meanings of these words.

For below-level students, preteach the sound /or/. Say several other words that include this sound, such as *corner, horn,* and *corn.* Ask students to repeat each word as you say it.

PHOTO CREDIT: C SQUARED STUDIOS/PHOTODISC/PICTUREQUEST

order

biggest

bigger

big

Unit 3
Sort and Classify

graph

Activating Prior Knowledge

Share Math Card 26 with students. Ask them to look closely at the card and describe what they see. Tell students that the picture is of a bar graph. Explain to students that there are different kinds of graphs. There are pie graphs, line graphs, picture graphs, and bar graphs. Discuss with students the importance of graphs. Tell them that a graph is a way to show information. Ask students to look at the bar graph in the picture about pets. Discuss how each graph always has a title. In this case, the title is underneath the graph. Explain to students that this graph will tell us what kind of pet most people prefer. Read the title of the graph to students. Talk about the different pets that are in the graph. Discuss how many people prefer each animal. Discuss with students the information that is shown on the graph; for example, which is the most preferred pet, and what is the least preferred pet.

Language Development

Show the card to students again. Ask students what letter the word at the top of the card begins with. They should answer "g." Ask what sounds are heard at the beginning of *graph*. While pointing to the word *graph*, read it out loud to students. Then point to the word while students read it with you. Read the word very slowly, "g-r-a-ph," and ask students to repeat it the same way. Talk about the sound that "g" and "r" make when they are put together. Tell them we call two letters together that make a specific sound a blend. Now, segment the word *graph*, "gr-a-ph" and have the students say it back to you. Ask them to think of other words that begin with the /gr/ sound. Make a list of words beginning with "gr" on the board. Some examples are *great, group, grunt,* and *grip.* Look at the sentence

at the bottom of the card. Ask students if they see any words in the sentence that they already know. Point to the words and read the sentence to students first and then have them read it with you.

Building Knowledge and Comprehension

Read the word *graph* at the top of the card and read the sentence at the bottom of the card with students. Ask a few students to come to the front and take turns pointing to the words while the rest of the class reads the sentence. Discuss with students the pets that they have at their homes. Tell students that you are going to make a class graph showing who has what pet at their homes, and who has no pet at all. Before class, prepare a graph using a large sheet of chart paper and a colored marker. Your graph should have six columns, one each for the following words: *cat, dog, bird, fish, other,* and *no pet.* Give each student a 2" x 2" (6 cm x 6 cm) piece of construction paper to glue in the appropriate column. Have each student write his or her name on the paper before gluing it on the graph. After all students have glued their piece of paper in the column showing the pets they have at their homes, discuss the graph. Talk about what pet is most common and what pet is least common.

Time to Differentiate!

For English language learners, preteach the vocabulary needed to discuss graphs. Write these words on the card.

For below-level students, preteach the /gr/ sound. Say the sound and have students repeat it after you. Say several other words that begin with the /gr/ sound, such as *great* and *grip.*

PHOTO CREDITS: © 2002 PHOTODISC

graph

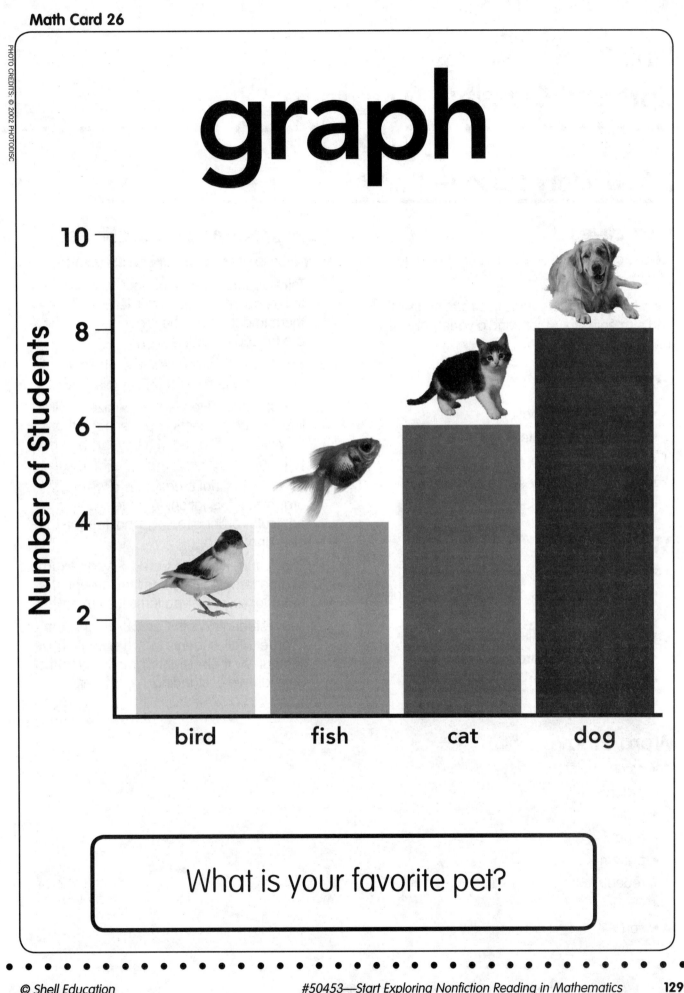

Number of Students

10

8

6

4

2

bird   fish   cat   dog

What is your favorite pet?

Unit 3
Sort and Classify

Introductory Lesson—Part A

Objectives

Pre-K Standard 6.1: Students know the sequence of events.

K–2 Standard 7.1: Students use reading skills and strategies to understand a variety of informational texts.

Skills

- organizing information
- recognizing a pattern
- recognizing a graph
- recognizing shapes
- making a pattern

Materials

- Math Cards 23–26
- various examples of graphs (bar, line, pie or pictograph)
- chalkboard or whiteboard
- chalk or whiteboard markers
- chart paper
- markers

Word Study

- category
- graph
- order
- organize
- pattern
- repeat
- shape
- sort

Comprehension and Skills

Part 1: Lesson Length: approx. 15 minutes

1. Tell students that you are going to ask them to line up in a particular order. Challenge them to determine the order in which they are placed in the line.

2. Call students to line up using an especially obvious pattern, such as boy-girl-boy-girl.

3. Ask students, "How did I organize you in line?" Lead students to understand that they were organized in a boy-girl-boy-girl pattern.

4. Tell students that a pattern is a way to organize information. A pattern is a particular order of objects that repeats itself over and over again.

5. Show students Math Card 24 as an example of a pattern. Ask them to look around the room for any other patterns they might see.

6. Show students Math Card 25 as an example of order. Tell students that they could have lined up by their heights, and this would be an example of standing in an order.

Introductory Lesson—Part A *(cont.)*

Comprehension and Skills

Part 2: Lesson Length: approx. 15 minutes

1. Show students Math Card 26. Explain that the card shows a graph. Ask, "What is a graph?" Make sure that they understand that a graph is another way to organize information. A graph is easy to read and understand just by looking at it.

2. Show the various examples of graphs to students. Call each by its name. Compare and contrast the different features of each graph.

3. Ask, "Have you ever seen a graph?" Let students share their experiences with graphs.

Comprehension and Skills

Part 3: Lesson Length: approx. 15 minutes

1. Show students Math Card 23. Tell them that this card shows three shapes. Ask students to help you review the three shapes pictured on the card. (Students might be able to mention other shapes that are not pictured, as well.)

2. Ask students to look around the room to find examples of these three shapes.

3. Point out that the shapes are also different colors. There is a blue square, a green triangle, and a pink circle.

4. Write the word *sort* on the board. Explain that sorting means to place objects in different categories. Give examples of how to sort using the students themselves. (They can be sorted by gender, hair color, clothing, etc. Be sure to use categories that do not embarrass students.)

Assessment

Have students help you create a pattern on a sheet of chart paper. (Choose a simple pattern, such as an ABAB pattern.) Ask students to decide on two shapes. Each shape should be drawn using a different colored marker. Have students tell you which shape to draw to keep the pattern going.

Unit 3
Sort and Classify

Focus Lesson

Objectives

Pre-K Standard 6.1: Students know the sequence of events.

K–2 Standard 7.1: Students use reading skills and strategies to understand a variety of informational texts.

Skills

- organizing information
- sorting objects
- recognizing a pattern
- creating a pattern
- recognizing a graph
- creating a graph
- reading and locating information on a graph

Materials

- Math Cards 23, 24, and 26
- different objects to show a pattern
- examples of a bar, line, pie, and pictograph
- large piece of chart paper and marker
- math manipulatives (different colors and different shapes)

Word Study

- category
- favorite
- graph
- order
- organize
- pattern
- pet
- repeat
- shape
- sort

Comprehension and Skills

Part 1: Lesson Length: approx. 15 minutes

1. Show students Math Card 24. Point out the word at the top of the card. Say, "This word starts with a 'p.' What sound does 'p' make?" Direct all students to make the /p/ sound.

2. Ask, "What word do you think this might be?" Lead students to understand that the word is *pattern*.

3. Point out the question at the bottom of the card. Ask, "Do you recognize any words that you see in the box?" Point to each word, the letters, and letter sounds, and have students help you read the question aloud.

4. Ask, "How is the picture on Math Card 24 organized?" Show students the pattern in the picture on Math Card 24. Share the pattern by saying it aloud while pointing to the objects (yellow flower, yellow flower, purple flower, yellow flower, yellow flower, purple flower, etc.).

Focus Lesson *(cont.)*

Comprehension and Skills

Part 2: Lesson Length: approx. 20 minutes

1. Tell students that they are going to help you organize objects in the same order as the flowers on Math Card 24. Ask students to help you recreate the same AABAAB pattern. When you are finished, check your pattern against the one shown on the card.

2. Ask, "Can anyone else choose two objects and create the same pattern?" Let students volunteer to create this pattern. Assist them in any way necessary. (If an AABAAB pattern is too difficult for students, help them to create an ABAB pattern.)

Comprehension and Skills

Part 3: Lesson Length: approx. 20 minutes

1. Show students Math Card 26. Help them sound out the word *graph*. Explain that a graph is another way to organize information. Review and name various examples of graphs.

2. Read the question on the bottom of Math Card 26. Model how you might read the graph. Share the data and explain how many people voted for each animal as their favorite pet. Remind them that you can understand the graph just by looking at it.

3. Tell students that a graph is an easy way to organize and show information to a reader. Select a favorite subject and poll students to get their data.

4. Use a sheet of blank chart paper to create a graph that resembles the one on Math Card 26. Place students' responses on the graph in the appropriate place.

Comprehension and Skills

Part 4: Lesson Length: approx. 20 minutes

1. Show students Math Card 23. Point out the word at the top of the card. Review the /sh/ digraph. Read each word on Math Card 23 as a group.

2. Tell students that some objects can be sorted by shape. Review the meaning of *sort*.

3. Choose a category and sort students according to that category (e.g., gender, hair color, height). Explain how you are sorting students while you are doing it. ("I am going to sort you by putting boys over here and girls over there.")

4. Do another sorting activity. Use math manipulatives to sort by color, size, or shape. If possible, do this activity without revealing the category and ask students, "What do all of these objects have in common? How are they different from this group of objects?"

Time to Differentiate!

For above-level students, provide them with a group of objects. Ask them to sort the objects several different ways.

Assessment

Place students in pairs. Ask them to create a pattern with their partner using objects in the classroom. When each pair is finished, they may share their patterns with the rest of the class.

Unit 3
Sort and Classify

Center Activities

Objectives

Pre-K Standard 6.1: Students know the sequence of events.

K–2 Standard 7.1: Students use reading skills and strategies to understand a variety of informational texts.

Center #1: Shape Sort

Materials

- Math Card 23
- different sizes of colored paper in the shape of squares, triangles, and circles
- student copies of Activity 23 (page 144)

Comprehension and Skills

1. Show students Math Card 23. Review the three shapes on Math Card 23: circle, square, and triangle.

2. Tell students that they will get to organize, or sort, objects using different categories.

3. Place the colored paper shapes in the center area. There should be a mixed pile of shapes for each student at the center. Model how they might begin to sort objects in different ways.

4. Tell students that they must check with an adult each time they have finished sorting the shapes in one way. (They can sort by size, shape, and color.) Then the adult will instruct them to continue to sort the objects by another category.

5. When students are finished sorting the shapes, they may complete Activity 23 (page 144). Read the directions aloud to students.

Center Activities *(cont.)*

Center #2:
Paper Patterns

Materials

- math manipulatives (tiles, cubes, blocks, etc.)
- student copies of Activity 24 (page 145)
- paper with a line drawn horizontally across the middle of the page
- crayons, markers, or colored pencils

Comprehension and Skills

1. Tell students that they will be creating a pattern at the center area. They will choose a pattern and create it with math manipulatives.

2. Once students have created a pattern, an adult can check to make sure it is a true pattern. After checking with an adult, the student will re-create the pattern on paper. Give each student a piece of drawing paper with a line drawn horizontally across the middle of the page so that they can keep the pattern organized on one line.

3. When they are finished, they may work on Activity 24 (page 145).

Center #3:
Graphs

Materials

- Math Card 26
- student copies of Activity 26 (page 147)
- pencils

Comprehension and Skills

1. Review Math Card 26 with students. Review how to read information on the graph.

2. At the center area, students may complete Activity 26 (page 147). Read the directions aloud to students.

Unit 3
Sort and Classify

Introductory Lesson—Part B

Objectives

Pre-K Standard 6.5: Students relate stories to their own lives and experiences.

K–2 Standard 5.1: Students use mental images based on pictures and print to aid in comprehension of text.

Skills

- connecting prior knowledge to text
- creating visual images
- recognizing shapes
- distinguishing different-sized objects
- understanding patterns

Materials

- Math Cards 24 and 25
- chalkboard or whiteboard
- chalk or whiteboard markers

Word Study

- imagine
- large
- order
- pattern
- shapes
- small

Comprehension and Skills

Part 1: Lesson Length: approx. 15 minutes

1. Start the lesson by asking students to help you list different kinds of shapes. Write each shape name on the board.

2. Say, "When you know about something, you can often picture it in your mind. Look at each shape on the list. Close your eyes and picture, or imagine, what each shape looks like." Draw the shape next to each written item on the list.

Comprehension and Skills

Part 2: Lesson Length: approx. 15 minutes

1. Show students Math Card 25, so they can see examples of different sizes of objects.

2. Now ask students to imagine a very large shape, such as a circle. Tell them to picture in their minds what a very large circle might look like. Then ask students to think of a very small circle. Finally, ask them to think of a medium-size circle. Tell them to imagine these shapes in order from smallest to biggest. Explain the distinctions between *large* and *small*.

Introductory Lesson—Part B *(cont.)*

Comprehension and Skills

Part 3: Lesson Length: approx. 20 minutes

1. Show students Math Card 24. Remind them of the definition of *pattern*.

2. Say, "Think of what you know about patterns. How can we make a pattern in this class?" Instruct students to look around the classroom to determine what might be used to make a pattern.

3. Let students use their prior knowledge of patterns and suggest ideas to the rest of the class.

Assessment

Ask students to share a time when they placed different-sized objects in order from smallest to largest or in a pattern. Students may share their experiences with a partner or during a whole class discussion.

Unit 3
Sort and Classify

Focus Lesson

Objectives

Pre-K Standard 6.5: Students relate stories to their own lives and experiences.

K–2 Standard 5.1: Students use mental images based on pictures and print to aid in comprehension of text.

Skills

- connecting prior knowledge to a text
- creating visual images
- reviewing the five senses

Materials

- Math Cards 23, 24, 25
- one read-aloud book
- chart paper
- marker
- objects that exemplify *big*, *bigger*, and *biggest*

Word Study

- familiar
- imagine
- order
- pattern
- sense
- shapes
- visualize

Comprehension and Skills

Part 1: Lesson Length: approx. 15 minutes

1. Find a read-aloud book to share with students. It should be a book that contains a sufficient amount of text and detail.

2. Tell students that there might be familiar things in this story. Explain that *familiar* describes something that they know about or have already learned.

3. Begin reading the story aloud. As you are reading, stop to ask students about various aspects of the story, including the characters, plot, and setting. The following questions may help them connect their prior knowledge to the elements of the text:

   - Does this character remind you of someone you know?
   - Has this ever happened to you before?
   - Have you ever been to a place like the one in the story?

Comprehension and Skills

Part 2: Lesson Length: approx. 20 minutes

1. Display Math Card 23. Review the word *shapes* with students and talk about its letters and letter sounds. Ask students to help you read *square, triangle*, and *circle* aloud.

2. Ask students, "What do you know about these three shapes?" Go through each shape, one at a time.

Focus Lesson *(cont.)*

3. As you discuss each shape, ask, "Where have you seen this shape before?"

4. Point to each picture on Math Card 23. Ask questions about the pictures to help activate students' five senses. Some questions might be the following:
   - What does a triangle instrument sound like?
   - What kind of weather might it be outside?
   - How does the round tube feel on her arms?
   - What do you think the young boy sees out the window?

Comprehension and Skills

Part 3: Lesson Length: approx. 20 minutes

1. Display Math Card 25. Review the word *order* with students and talk about its letters and letter sounds. Since *order* can have several definitions, talk about what *order* means in this context.

2. Ask students to help you sound out *big*, *bigger*, and *biggest*. Show them that *bigger* and *biggest* have endings, or suffixes, that change the meaning of the word.

3. Ask, "What objects do you know that also could be pictured on Math Card 25?" Model several appropriate responses, and then ask students to share their own ideas.

4. If possible, find objects around the classroom that might also be categorized as *big*, *bigger*, and *biggest*.

Comprehension and Skills

Part 4: Lesson Length: approx. 20 minutes

1. Display Math Card 24. Review the word *pattern* with students. Point out the sentence in the box, and ask students to help you read it aloud.

2. Look closely at the pattern picture. Review the pattern, if necessary.

3. Ask the following questions to help activate students' senses:
   - What do you think these flowers might smell like?
   - How would they feel if you could touch them?
   - What colors do you see?
   - What shapes do you see in the flowers?

4. Discuss students' prior knowledge of flowers. Ask, "Where do you see flowers growing? What are your favorite flowers?"

Time to Differentiate!

For above-level students, have students create riddles for an object in the classroom. Remind them to give clues that address the senses.

Assessment

Send students on a scavenger hunt around the classroom. Ask them to find five objects:
- something that is in the shape of a circle, triangle, or square
- something that can be described using the five senses
- three objects that are big, bigger, and biggest

Unit 3
Sort and Classify

Center Activities

Objectives

Pre-K Standard 6.5: Students relate stories to their own lives and experiences.

K–2 Standard 5.1: Students use mental images based on pictures and print to aid in comprehension of text.

Center #1: Shape Pictures

Materials

- Math Card 23
- colored construction paper
- paper cut into shapes in various colors and sizes
- glue sticks

Comprehension and Skills

1. Review shapes with students by showing them Math Card 23.

2. Remind students of the objects in the classroom that resemble certain shapes. Tell students that there are many things in the world that also resemble certain shapes.

3. Show students the colored construction paper. Then show them the paper that has been cut into different shapes in various colors and sizes.

4. Model how students can use the paper shapes to create a picture. It can look like anything that they imagine, or visualize, while looking at shapes. It might be a picture of a real object, such as a house, or it can be an abstract picture that resembles a real object.

5. Show students how they can use a glue stick to glue the shapes onto the colored construction paper.

6. Place these materials in the center area. Students can work on this project independently.

7. Display the finished products in a prominent place in the classroom.

Center Activities *(cont.)*

Center #2:
Big, Bigger, Biggest

Materials

- Math Card 25
- drawing paper
- crayons, markers, or colored pencils
- student copies of Activity 25 (page 146)

Comprehension and Skills

1. Review order with students by showing them Math Card 25.

2. Ask students to think of objects that they would like to draw to show *big*, *bigger*, and *biggest*. If you are studying a specific topic, such as weather or oceans, you can have each student use that topic for this project. You may even tie the center to a recent holiday.

3. Leave Math Card 25, drawing paper, and coloring materials at the center area. Students can work on this project independently.

4. When students are finished, they may work on Activity 25 (page 146).

Unit 3
Sort and Classify

Wrap-up

Introduction

The wrap-up activities tie together the skills that have been taught throughout the unit. They provide opportunities for students to show the skills they have learned within this unit.

Objectives

Pre-K Standard 6.1: Students know the sequence of events.

Pre-K Standard 6.5: Students relate stories to their own lives and experiences.

K–2 Standard 5.1: Students use mental images based on pictures and print to aid in comprehension of text.

K–2 Standard 7.1: Students use reading skills and strategies to understand a variety of informational texts.

Materials

- Math Cards 23–26
- various shapes in different colors and sizes of paper

Comprehension and Skills

Part 1: Lesson Length: approx. 15 minutes

1. Show Math Cards 23–26 to students.

2. Go through each card one at a time. Ask students to help you read the text on each card. They should be familiar with the titles and text on each page.

3. Ask questions about the meaning of each card's title. (What is a pattern? What shapes do you know? What is a graph? How would you explain order?)

4. Talk about how each topic is related to their lives. (What shapes do you see in the world? What patterns exist in your house? When have you seen a graph before? What objects can represent the ideas of big, bigger, and biggest?)

5. Talk about the visual images associated with each card's topic.

Wrap-up *(cont.)*

Comprehension and Skills

Part 2: Lesson Length: approx. 20 minutes

1. Ask students to sit in a circle. Place the paper shapes in the middle of the circle. Scatter the shapes so that they are not placed on top of each other.

2. Ask two students to go in the middle of the circle to find all the squares.

3. Ask two more students to find all the circles.

4. Ask two more students to find all the triangles.

5. Have students place all the shapes back in the circle.

6. Ask two students to go in the middle of the circle to find all the shapes that might be considered the biggest shapes.

7. Ask two more students to go in the middle of the circle to find all the shapes that might be considered the bigger shapes.

8. Have students place those shapes back in the circle. Ask other students to make a pattern using the shapes.

9. Each student should be able to show a different pattern. It might be a pattern of color, size, or shape.

Unit 3
Sort and Classify

Name _____

Color these **shapes** in the picture: 8 squares, 6 circles, 3 triangles.

© Shell Education

Name _____

Sort and Classify

Find the **pattern** in each row. Draw the next shape in the **pattern**.

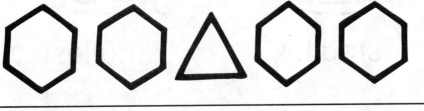

Make your own **pattern**. Ask a friend to continue the **pattern** on a sheet of paper.

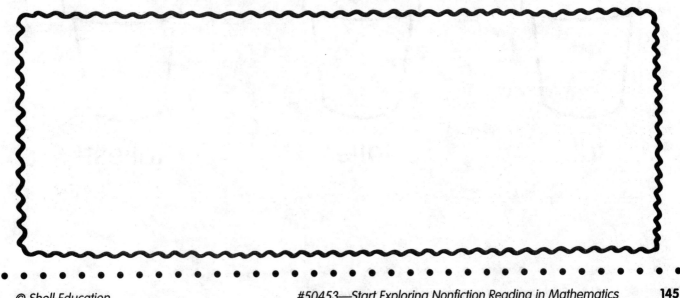

Unit 3

Sort and Classify

Name _____

Draw a picture to finish each row.

small

smaller

smallest

tall

taller

tallest

Name _____

Look at the **graph** to answer the questions.

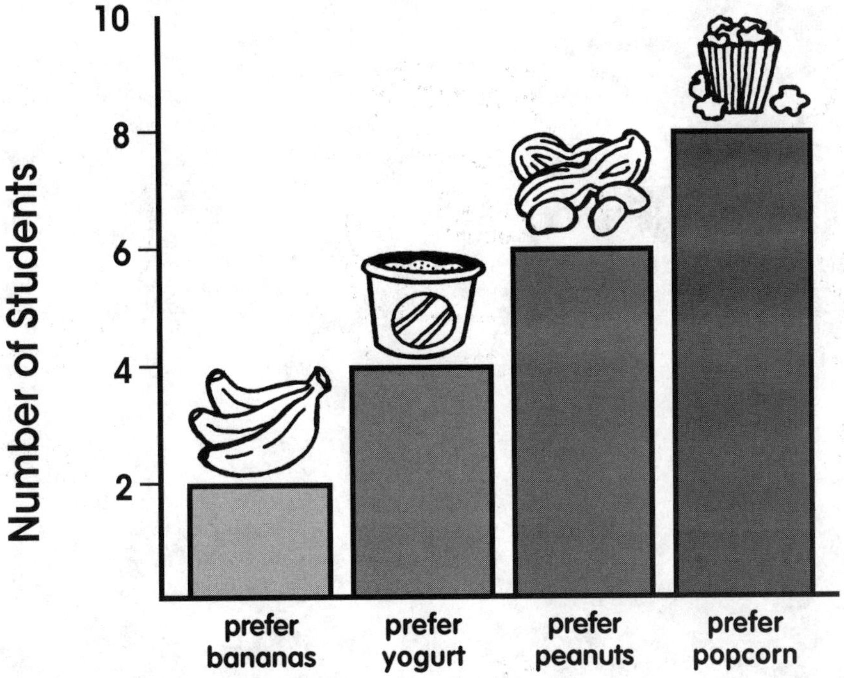

Which snack do most people like?

_____

_____

Which snack do the fewest people like?

_____

_____

On the back, make your own **graph**. Ask your friends and family to name their favorite colors. Put the information in a **graph**.

Numbers

Operations

Sort and Classify

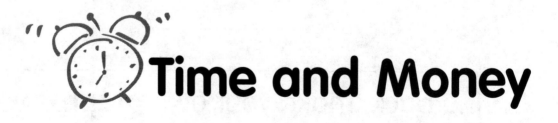

Time and Money

Introduction to Unit 4: Time and Money

This unit introduces students to the important concepts of time and money. Students will become familiar with understanding that different activities happen at different times of the day. They will also learn how to count different types of money. Important vocabulary terms such as *buy*, *cents*, *coin*, *reaction*, *clock*, *hour*, *minute*, *question*, and *statement* are also introduced. In this unit, students will learn to use reading stategies such as asking questions to comprehend new information.

Skills Taught in This Unit

- reacting to text
- understanding reactions to various topics
- sharing reactions orally with classmates
- distinguishing between questions and statements
- understanding questions that are raised by a reader
- asking questions

Directions for the Teacher

You have many different options when teaching this unit. You can use the nonfiction text pages (Math Cards) and teach the content using the strategies that precede each card. Or, you can teach nonfiction skills and strategies by teaching the whole unit, starting with the introductory lesson, then teaching the focus lesson, and then following up with the center activities. This format repeats for the second lesson in the unit. Conclude the unit by teaching the wrap-up activity to tie all the nonfiction text and skills together.

Unit 4
Time and Money

money

Activating Prior Knowledge

Share Math Card 27 with students. Ask them to describe what they see. Tell students that the money pictured is United States currency. Ask students to think about why we need money. Write their comments on the board or a piece of chart paper. Discuss each piece of currency pictured, beginning with the penny. Discuss who is pictured on the penny and why he is important. Talk about how much a penny is worth and what a person could buy with a penny. Continue to discuss each piece of currency and whose picture is on it. If possible, have examples of all of the money for students to touch and examine. Have a large amount of play money available for students to sort and classify in small groups. They could also make patterns with the money. For example, penny, dime, penny, dime, penny, dime.

Language Development

Ask students to look at the card and describe what they see. Direct their attention to the word *money* at the top of the card. Tell them the word is *money* and ask them what letter it begins with. After they tell you it begins with the letter "m," ask them to practice making the /m/ sound. Ask students to look at the word *money* and see if they recognize what letters are vowels. Direct students' attention to the sentence at the bottom of the card. Tell them to look carefully and see if they recognize any words in the sentence. While pointing to the words, read the sentence to students. Ask students to read the sentence with you several more times while you point to the words. While reading the sentence, show an action while reading the word *money*. Students can clap their hands, stomp their feet, or snap their fingers.

Building Knowledge and Comprehension

Find a copy of money that can be run on construction paper. Enlarge the money so it is easy for students to recognize. For example, the nickel should be about six inches (18cm) in diameter. You should have approximately four quarters, 10 dimes, 10 nickels, and 31 pennies. Laminate the paper coins and attach a magnet to the back. Ask students to read the word *money* and the sentence at the bottom of the card while you point to the words. Tell them that you are going to help them learn the value of a penny, nickel, dime, and quarter. For example, if it is the sixth day of the month, there should be six pennies on the board. Continue to follow this same process for each day of the month, adding a penny each day. Start out using pennies and gradually introduce the remaining coins when appropriate. For example, use pennies the first month, pennies and nickels the second month, and so on.

Time to Differentiate!

For English language learners, preteach the names of the various pieces of currency. For example, *penny*, *nickel*, *dime*, *quarter*, and *dollar bill*. Write these words on the board as you show students each one.

For below-level students, provide additional practice with making several versions of an ABAB pattern. Use various objects from the classroom.

 © Shell Education

PHOTO CREDIT: 1,5,10 DOLLAR BILLS: PHOTOSPIN, DIME,PENNY, QUARTER: © 2002 PHOTODISC

money

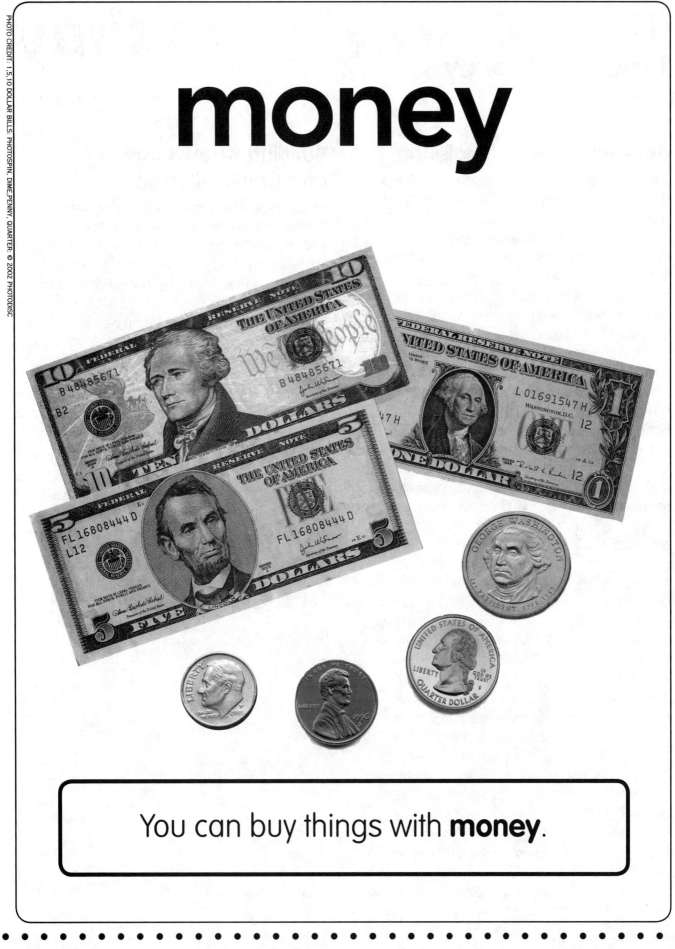

You can buy things with **money**.

Unit 4
Time and Money

time

Activating Prior Knowledge

Share with students Math Card 28. Ask them to describe what they see. Tell them that the picture is of Big Ben, a very famous clock tower in London, England. If possible, have a teaching clock for students to look at. Ask them to describe what they see on a clock. Talk about the numbers, how many seconds make a minute, how many minutes make an hour, the minute hand, and the second hand. Ask students to say the numbers on the clock as you point to them. Talk about how the minute hand moves quicker and is longer than the hour hand, and that it takes an hour for the hour hand to move to the next number. Explain how every time the minute hand moves to a new number, five minutes have passed. Ask students to practice counting by fives as you move the minute hand around the clock. Practice telling time by the hour, moving the minute hand around the clock before starting the next hour.

Language Development

Show students the card. Ask them again to describe what they see in the picture. Tell them that the word at the top of the card is *time*. Ask them to name the first letter of the word *time*. After they respond that the word *time* begins with the letter "t," ask them to practice making the /t/ sound. Ask students to think of other words that begin with the letter "t." Write the "t" words on the board or a sheet of chart paper. Direct students' attention to the sentence at the bottom of the card. Ask them if they recognize any words in the sentence. Point to the words and read the sentence. Ask students to read the sentence with you several more times while you point to the words. Students could take turns pointing to the words while the remainder of the class reads the sentence out loud.

Building Knowledge and Comprehension

Show students the card. Ask them to read the word *time* at the top of the card as you point to it. Ask them to read the sentence at the bottom of the card as you point to it. Ask students to clap their hands when they read the word *time*. Tell students that they are going to keep track of time throughout the day. Set an alarm clock so that it rings on the hour (and half hour, if desired). When the alarm sounds, have students tell the time. If a set of student clocks with movable hands is available, have students manipulate the clock hands to match the time on the hour (or half hour).

Time to Differentiate!

For English language learners, preteach the language needed for these lesson. Discuss the words *minutes, hours, clock,* etc. Model how to tell time by the hour.

For below-level students, preteach how to count the minutes and hours on a clock. Use sticky notes to label a clock with the minutes. Model how to tell time by the hour. Practice counting by fives.

PHOTO CREDIT: (BIG BEN) CORBIS IMAGES/PICTUREQUEST, (SMALL BLUE) © 2002 PHOTODISC

time

Can you tell what **time** it is?

Unit 4
Time and Money

Introductory Lesson—Part A

Objective
Pre-K and K–2 Standard 6.5: Students relate stories to their own lives and personal experiences.

Skills
- reacting to text
- understanding reactions to various topics

Materials
- Math Card 27
- dollar bills
- coins of each denomination
- chalkboard or whiteboard
- chalk or whiteboard markers
- drawing paper
- crayons, markers, or colored pencils
- pencils

Word Study
- buy
- cents
- coin
- dollar bill
- money
- reaction

Comprehension and Skills

Part 1: Lesson Length: approx. 15 minutes

1. Ask students, "When you see a friend crying or hurt in some way, how do you feel?" Let students orally share their experiences and feelings in response to the question.

2. Write the word *reaction* on the board. Tell students that a reaction is how you feel or respond to something you experience. Tell them that they might react to an event that they see or hear, to what other people say or do, or even to something they read or see in a book or other text.

3. Choose an emotion and ask a question to get students thinking about a reaction they have had in their lives. The question might sound like the following example: "When was the last time that something or someone made you feel scared?"

4. Let students answer the question above and share their experience with the rest of the class.

Introductory Lesson—Part A *(cont.)*

Comprehension and Skills

Part 2: Lesson Length: approx. 20 minutes

1. Give each student a sheet of drawing paper and coloring materials. Students should draw a picture of a time when they reacted by feeling scared, excited, angry, happy, or nervous.

2. Then students can write any words they know to describe what is going on in the picture. An adult can also take dictation and write a sentence to describe the picture.

3. Share these pictures with the class. Explain that each of their experiences from the pictures is an example of how they reacted to something with a particular emotion.

Comprehension and Skills

Part 3: Lesson Length: approx. 20 minutes

1. Show the students real dollar bills and coins. Ask them to help you make a list of words on the board that refer to money in the United States. Make sure to include words such as dollar bill, coin, cash, cents, and money.

2. If possible, pass around the bills and coins so that students can look closely at money.

3. Ask students the following questions:

   • Why do we need money?

   • What does it mean to buy something?

   • Have you ever wanted something but do not have enough money to buy it?

   • Have you ever been given money and were able to decide how to spend it on your own? What did you buy?

   • What can you have that does not cost any money?

Comprehension and Skills

Part 4: Lesson Length: approx. 20 minutes

1. Show students Math Card 27. Point to the word *money* at the top of the card. Say, "This word starts with an 'm.' What sound does 'm' make?" Have students say the sound.

2. Ask, "Do you recognize any other letters in this word? Look at the picture. What do you think this word might be?" Lead students to understand that the word is *money*.

3. Point out each dollar bill and coin on Math Card 27. Everything that is pictured on the card is called money. Identify each bill and coin by its name and its value. After you say each name, have students repeat it.

4. Read the sentence at the bottom of the card. Ask students, "What is something you have bought with money?" Let students share their responses with the rest of the class.

Assessment

Ask students, "What is the definition of reaction?" Let them share their answers with a partner. You may also ask students to help you list different names for various kinds of money. As students volunteer information, write it on the board.

Unit 4
Time and Money

Focus Lesson

Objective

Pre-K and K–2 Standard 6.5: Students relate stories to their own lives and personal experiences.

Skills

- reacting to text
- sharing reactions orally with classmates

Materials

- Math Card 27
- read-aloud book
- chalkboard or whiteboard
- chalk or whiteboard markers
- drawing paper
- crayons, markers, or colored pencils
- an additional read-aloud book (see Assessment)

Word Study

- amount
- buy
- emotion
- feelings
- money
- reaction

Comprehension and Skills

Part 1: Lesson Length: approx. 15 minutes

1. Choose a story to read aloud to students. Find a story that will likely evoke a particular emotion in them as they listen. It might be a story that makes students feel scared, sad, confused, worried, happy, amused, etc.

2. Show students the cover of the book. Read aloud the title and author's name. Tell students that you are going to read the story aloud. Comment that stories will often make readers feel a particular kind of emotion. This feeling is known as a reaction. Talk about what an emotion is.

3. Discuss different kinds of emotions, or feelings, and list them on the board. Draw a face next to each word on the list to show what the feeling might look like.

4. Tell students that you want them to think about what emotion they feel as you read the story.

5. Begin to read the story aloud. As you are reading, stop at certain points throughout the story to ask students, "How are you reacting to this part of the story? What emotions are you feeling?" Discuss their answers as a group. Be sure to model responses and share your reactions to the story.

Focus Lesson *(cont.)*

Comprehension and Skills

Part 2: Lesson Length: approx. 20 minutes

1. Show students Math Card 27.

2. Ask, "What do you feel when you see the money on this card? What is your reaction?" These questions might be too abstract for students to understand because Math Card 27 does not carry the strong meaning that a story and characters can. It might be helpful to prompt students with specific questions that will reference their reactions. Some questions might be the following:

   - Does this look like a large or small amount of money?

   - How much money do you think you see?

   - Have you ever had this much money?

   - Where might you get this kind of money?

   - If you had this money, what would you buy?

   - What could you not buy with this much money?

3. Let students answer these questions and share their reactions with the rest of the class.

Comprehension and Skills

Part 3: Lesson Length: approx. 20 minutes

1. Distribute drawing paper and coloring materials. Ask students to draw a picture of what they might buy if they had the amount of money on Math Card 27.

2. Let students share their pictures with the rest of the class.

Time to Differentiate!

For above-level students, have them work in small groups to act out a short story about buying the items they drew in Part 3 of the lesson.

Assessment

Choose another story to share with students. Read the story aloud. When you are finished reading, ask students to sit with a partner to talk about how they felt about the book and why. Model your reaction first before asking students to talk with partners to share their reactions.

Unit 4
Time and Money

• •

Center Activities

Objective

Pre-K and K–2 Standard 6.5: Students relate stories to their own lives and personal experiences.

Center #1:
Shopping for Toys

Materials

- crayons, markers, or colored pencils
- drawing paper
- cards showing pictures of various toys
- index cards (optional, see step 1)

Comprehension and Skills

1. To explain this activity, show each card to students. Tell them that each card shows a picture of a toy that might be found in a toy store. (If you don't have cards that show pictures of toys, an option would be to have each student draw a picture of his or her favorite toy on an index card. These pictures could then be used in this center activity.)

2. Tell students that when people go to shop and spend money, they have reactions, or feelings, to things they see in stores. They might feel strongly about something and want to buy it, they might dislike an object and not consider buying it, or they might have no reaction to a product.

3. Ask students to imagine going into a toy store with money in their pocket to spend on five toys. They must imagine that the toys pictured on the cards are the toys that they find in a toy store. Students have to choose which five toys they might buy with the money they have.

4. Remind students that they will be making choices about each toy based on their reactions to the picture. In other words, if they have a positive reaction to the toy, they might decide to "buy" it. If they have a negative reaction, they will not choose to purchase that toy.

5. Show each card to the class and call each toy by its name. Make sure that students are somewhat familiar with most of the toys on the cards.

6. At the center area, leave drawing paper and coloring materials. Instruct students to look through the cards independently. They should make their five choices, draw their picks on drawing paper, and color them.

• •

Center Activities *(cont.)*

Center #2:
Toy Identification

Materials

- student copies of Activity 27 (page 168)
- crayons, markers, or colored pencils
- pencils

Comprehension and Skills

1. When students are finished drawing their pictures, they may write letters or a word to identify each toy. (If the cards have the name of the toy already written on them, students may copy the word onto their own drawing paper to label each picture.)

2. As students finish, they may work on Activity 27 (page 168). This exercise can be done independently or with another student at the center who is also done with his or her work. Read the directions to students. Have them circle the correct amount of money for each toy. Then have students color their pages.

Unit 4
Time and Money

Introductory Lesson—Part B

Objectives

Pre-K Standard 5.8: Students know that print appears in different forms and serves different purposes.

K–2 Standard 7.1: Students use reading skills and strategies to understand a variety of informational texts.

Skills

- distinguishing between questions and statements
- understanding questions that are raised by a reader

Materials

- chalkboard or whiteboard
- chalk or whiteboard markers
- read-aloud book
- clock with movable hands
- 10–20 small clocks with movable hands
- chart paper and marker (see Assessment)

Word Study

- ask
- clock
- hour
- minute
- punctuation
- question
- statement
- time

Comprehension and Skills

Part 1: Lesson Length: approx. 15 minutes

1. Start the lesson with a discussion of the difference between a question and a statement.

2. Write the following statement and question on the board:
   - I like to ride my bike.
   - Do you know how to ride a bike?

3. Read each aloud. Then discuss the differences between a statement and a question. Point out the ending punctuation that indicates a statement or question in writing.

4. Make sure that students understand the definitions of both a question and a statement. (A question is a sentence that asks something, and a statement is a sentence that tells something.)

5. Ask students to think of a statement and a question example, such as the one you shared, and share it with the rest of the class. Continue doing this activity until all students have had a chance to share their examples with the class.

Introductory Lesson—Part B (cont.)

Comprehension and Skills

Part 2: Lesson Length: approx. 20 minutes

1. Find a read-aloud book to share with students. It should be a book that contains an interesting plot and several details throughout the book. It may be fiction or nonfiction.

2. Explain that readers will often ask questions while they are reading. They can ask questions about many different aspects of the story. Perhaps they wonder about a character or an event in the story. Readers might not know a particular word or phrase in the book. Maybe they will ask questions about why an author included certain information in the story.

3. Begin reading the book aloud. Use a think-aloud process while you are reading to share the questions you have with students. A think-aloud might sound like the following example:

   "One day a bear was walking in the woods. (Was the bear walking alone or with another bear?) He came across a stump. (What is a stump?) He wanted to sit down and take a rest. (Can bears really sit on stumps? Is this fiction or nonfiction?) Then he saw a beehive in a nearby tree. (Isn't he going to be interested in the bees' honey?)"

4. Continue reading the story aloud and sharing your questions and thoughts with students. It is important to point out that a reader might ask many questions about a story, but they won't always be answered by the story itself. Talk about which questions were answered by the story and which were not.

Comprehension and Skills

Part 3: Lesson Length: approx. 20 minutes

1. Show students a clock with movable hands. Ask them, "What am I holding?" Let student volunteers share their ideas with the rest of the class. If possible, pass out clocks for each student so that they can experiment with how a clock works.

2. Point out the numbers around the clock. Ask students to help you read each number, 1–12.

3. Discuss the importance of knowing what time it is. Ask questions such as:

   - Where have you seen a clock?
   - When is it important to know the time?

4. Briefly show students how the numbers on the clock correspond to the time of day. For example, the 12 on the clock represents 12:00, which can be noon or midnight. Talk about the differences between a.m. and p.m. (Do not try to teach students how to read a clock. Students may not be developmentally aware of how a clock works or how it indicates a passage of time.)

Assessment

Ask students to talk with a partner to share the differences between a statement and a question. Decide on two definitions as a group, and write them on the board or on chart paper.

Unit 4
Time and Money

Focus Lesson

Objectives

Pre-K Standard 5.8: Students know that print appears in different forms and serves different purposes.

K–2 Standard 7.1: Students use reading skills and strategies to understand a variety of informational texts.

Skills

- distinguishing between questions and statements
- asking questions

Materials

- Math Card 28
- 10–20 small clocks with movable hands
- read-aloud book (see Assessment)

Word Study

- ask
- clock
- hour
- minute
- question
- statement
- time

Comprehension and Skills

Part 1: Lesson Length: approx. 15 minutes

1. Review the differences between a statement and a question. Ask students to give examples of both.

2. Remind students that many readers ask questions while they are reading. Often, the reader will think of these questions in his or her head. Tell them that asking questions means that they are making a reading experience more personal and relevant because they are looking for answers to questions that are meaningful.

3. Show Math Card 28 to students.

4. Ask, "What does this picture show?" (a clock) Point to both clocks on the card. Tell students that one clock shows Roman numerals and one clock shows numbers with which they are familiar.

5. Point to the title of the card. Tell students that the word starts with "t." Ask, "What does a 't' sound like?" Have them make the sound together. Ask, "What might this word be?" If they do not recognize the word, read *time* aloud. Ask them to all repeat *time*.

6. Point to the sentence on Math Card 28. Ask students, "Do you recognize any words in the sentence?" Repeat the same process as above so that students can sound out the words on Math Card 28.

Focus Lesson (cont.)

Comprehension and Skills

Part 2: Lesson Length: approx. 15 minutes

1. Show students Math Card 28. Reread the sentence to students.

2. Distribute student clocks with movable hands. Students should show the same time on Math Card 28 on their own clock. Ask students if they can tell what time is shown on the clock. (Remember that the emphasis of this lesson is on reading skills, not on learning to tell time.) Let students share how they read a clock with other students.

3. Model how you might raise a question about Math Card 28. Some examples of questions are:

   - Where is this large clock located?
   - Is this a famous building?
   - Does the clock make a sound or chime at certain times?
   - Why does the clock use Roman numerals?
   - Can people climb to the top of the clock?
   - Do people actually use this clock to tell time?
   - Are there clocks on all four sides of the building?
   - What am I doing at this time of day?
   - Is this clock showing 5:00 in the morning or evening?

4. Let students share any other questions they have about Math Card 28. Remind them that these questions might require further research and reading in order to be answered. They might not be answered by reading Math Card 28.

Time to Differentiate!

For above-level students, have each one write one statement and one question to read to the class. Let each student lead the class in identifying whether it is a statement or question.

Assessment

Choose a story to read aloud. Let students stop you throughout the story to ask questions. When you are finished reading, talk as a group about which questions could be answered by the text and which require further reading.

Unit 4
Time and Money

Center Activities

Objectives

Pre-K Standard 5.8: Students know that print appears in different forms and serves different purposes.

K–2 Standard 7.1: Students use reading skills and strategies to understand a variety of informational texts.

Center #1: Telling Time

Materials

- drawing paper
- crayons, markers, or colored pencils
- clock with movable hands
- 10–20 small clocks with movable hands

Comprehension and Skills

1. Distribute clocks with movable hands to each student or each pair of students. Using your clock, model for students how to show 12:00. Ask students to show the same time on their own clocks.

2. Explain that when people see a clock and read the time, they will wonder what they are or should be doing at that time. Tell students that they are going to get to answer those types of questions.

3. Ask students questions such as, "What time might you wake up in the morning?" Model how they might show those times on a clock.

4. Show students a blank sheet of drawing paper. At the center, students will take a sheet of paper and fold it into four quarters. In each quarter of the paper, students will draw pictures of what they look like when they wake up in the morning, eat lunch, do homework, and go to bed.

5. If an adult is at the center, he or she might be able to help students write a word or phrase that describes what is shown in each picture. Also, a small clock could be added to each part of the page to indicate the time of the activity.

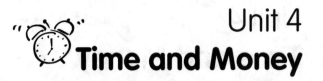
Center Activities *(cont.)*

Center #2: Clocks

Materials

- student copies of Activity 28 (page 169)
- pencils

Comprehension and Skills

1. Distribute Activity 28 (page 169) to students. Read the directions aloud.

2. Activity 28 shows four clocks. Students must answer questions such as, "What time might you wake up in the morning?" Model how they might show those times on a clock. Then model how they might indicate those times on the worksheet.

3. Students can draw hands on the clocks to describe the times they do each activity listed on the sheet.

4. Students may work on these pages independently or with a partner.

Unit 4
Time and Money

Wrap-Up

Introduction

The wrap-up activities tie together the skills that have been taught throughout the unit. They provide opportunities for students to show the skills they have learned within this unit.

Objectives

Pre-K Standard 5.8: Students know that print appears in different forms and serves different purposes.

Pre-K and K–2 Standard 6.5: Students relate stories to their own lives and personal experiences.

K–2 Standard 7.1: Students use reading skills and strategies to understand a variety of informational texts.

Materials

- read-aloud book
- Math Cards 27 and 28

Comprehension and Skills

Part 1: Lesson Length: approx. 15 minutes

1. Choose a story to read aloud to students. Find a story that will likely evoke a particular emotion in them as they listen.

2. Show students the cover of the book. Read aloud the title and author's name. Tell students that you are going to read the story aloud.

3. Tell students that you want them to think about what emotion they feel as you read the story.

4. Students should be able to share their reactions of the text with only short prompts from you, such as:
   - What do you think of this?
   - How does this make you feel?
   - What are you thinking right now?

5. When you are finished reading the story, ask students to share statements and questions about the story. The questions may or may not be answered by the text.

Wrap-up (cont.)

Comprehension and Skills

Part 2: Lesson Length: approx. 20 minutes

1. Display Math Cards 27 and 28. Have students read the titles and the sentences aloud as a group.

2. Have students focus on Math Card 27. As a class, count the money on the card. Have student volunteers discuss items they would like to buy if they had that amount of money.

3. Now, have students focus on Math Card 28. Ask the class to tell you what time is listed on the clock on the card. Have student volunteers discuss the activities they like to do at that time of day.

Unit 4
Time and Money

Name _____

How much **money** does each toy cost?

Circle the coins or bills you need to buy each toy.

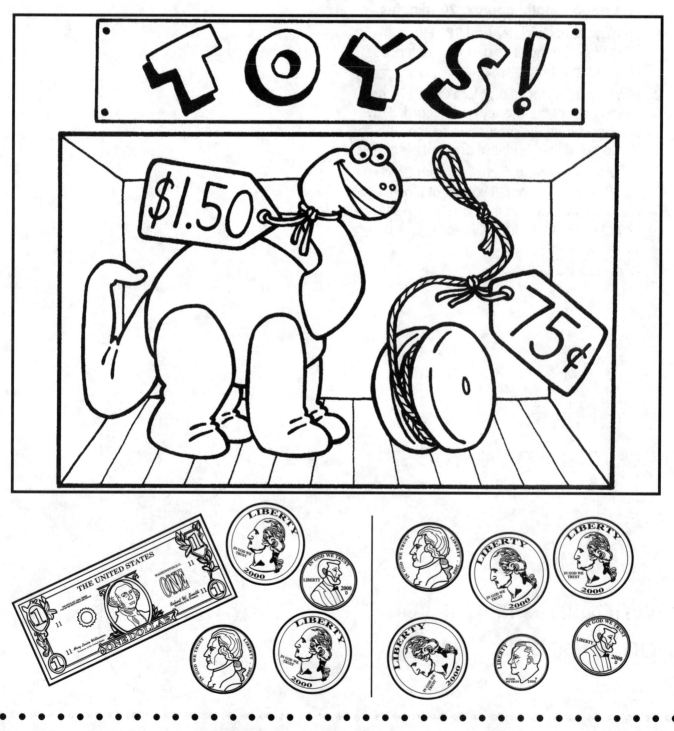

Name _____

Unit 4
Time and Money

Read the questions. Draw a hand on each clock to show the **time**.

What time might you wake up in the morning?

What time might you eat lunch?

What time might you do your homework?

What time might you go to bed?

References Cited

Berry, R. 2001. Children's environmental print: Reliability, validity, and relationship to early reading. Doctoral dissertation, University of North Carolina at Chapel Hill.

Christie, J. F., B. J. Enz, M. Gerard, and J. Prior. 2002. Using environmental print as teaching materials and assessment tools. Paper presented at the International Reading Association annual convention, San Francisco, CA.

Christie, J. F., B. J. Enz, and C. Vukelich. 2002. *Teaching language and literacy, preschool through the elementary grades.* 2nd. ed. New York: Longman.

Csikszentmihalyi, M. 1990. *Flow: The psychology of optimal experience.* New York: Harper & Row Publishers.

Duke, N. K., and V. Purcell-Gates. 2003. Genres at home and at school: Bridging the known to the new. *The Reading Teacher* 57 (1): 30–37.

Ferreiro, E., and A. Teberosky. 1982. *Literacy before schooling.* Exeter, NH: Heinemann.

Goodman, Y. 1986. Children coming to know literacy. In *Emergent literacy: Writing and reading,* ed., W. H. Teale and E. Sulzby, 1–14. Norwood, NJ: Ablex.

Harste, J., C. Burke, and V. Woodward. 1982. Children's language and world: Initial encounters with print. In *Reader meets author/bridging the gap: A psycholinguistic and sociolinguistic perspective,* ed. J. A. Langer and M. T. Smith-Burke, 105–31. Newark, DE: International Reading Association.

NAEYC. 2001. What does it look like and what does it take?: Supporting early literacy. White House Summit on Early Childhood Cognitive Development, Washington, D.C.

National Institute of Child Health and Human Development. 2000. *Teaching children to read: An evidence-based assessment of the scientific research literature on reading and its implications for reading instruction.* Report of the National Reading Panel. Washington, D.C.: U.S. Government Print Office.

Orellana, M. F., and A. Hernandez. 2003. Talking the walk: Children reading urban environmental print. In *Promising practices for urban reading instruction,* ed., P. A. Mason and J. S. Schumm, 25–36. Newark, DE: International Reading Association.

Piaget, J. 1978. *Success and understanding.* Cambridge, MA: Harvard University Press.

Simmons, D., B. Gunn, S. Smith, and E. J. Kame'enui. 1994. Phonological awareness: Application of instructional design. LD Forum 19 (2): 7–10.

Tomlinson, C. 2000. *Leadership for Differentiating Schools and Classrooms.* Alexandria, VA: Association for Supervision and Curriculum Development.

U.S. Department of Education. 2000. *No Child Left Behind.* http://www.ed.gov/nclb/landing.html

U.S. Department of Education. 2001. *Early Reading First.* http://www.ed.gov/programs/earlyreading/index.html

Xu, S. H., and A. L. Rutledge. 2003. Chicken starts with ch! Kindergartners learn through environmental print. *Young Children* 58 (2): 44–51.

Notes

Notes

© Shell Education

Notes

Notes

#50453—*Start Exploring Nonfiction Reading in Mathematics* © Shell Education

Notes

Notes